"In this book, Deborah Eden Tull offers the strong medicine of darkness, which helps us navigate the uncertainty of our times. The overlighting of our planet in its urban and more populated areas robs people of access to their own hidden depths, so needed in these times of growing peril."

—JOANNA MACY, author of *Active Hope*

"A novel and inspiring exploration of darkness bringing grace and balance to the complexity of our time." —RUTH KING, author of *Mindful of Race*

"*Luminous Darkness* is an extraordinary and profoundly clear exploration of the greatest divine mystery of all: that luminous darkness in which as Rumi said, 'the lovers drown themselves.' Reading the book is itself an initiation, and the rewards of the initiation are profounder strength, vaster awe, and ineradicable commitment to celebration and justice."

—ANDREW HARVEY, author of *The Hope* and *Engoldenment*

"Deborah Eden Tull skillfully illuminates the wonders of the dark, shedding light on areas of life where even angels fear to tread. Artificial light is destroying us, but the real light in this book can save us. By obeying the natural curfew of the night, and exploring the darkest corners of our mind, we can tap into natural resources previously buried in broad daylight. This book is a trustworthy guide to the treasures tucked within each of us." —ANDREW HOLECEK, author of *Dreams of Light*

"*Luminous Darkness* is a wise, beautiful, important book. Through personal story, deep dharma teachings, and social commentary, Deborah Eden Tull reclaims the power of darkness and the divine feminine and reweaves the often-overlooked threads—of potent mystery, fierce compassion, receptivity and relationship, imagination, and emergence—into the cloth of spiritual life. This is essential reading for anyone seeking to heal the wounds of inner and outer divisiveness and engage our wide, aching world with a radiant, tender heart." —PAMELA WEISS, author of *A Bigger Sky*

"From natural to social systems, *Luminous Darkness* illuminates with vivid imagery and sensory aliveness how reorienting and rebalancing ourselves inwardly is necessary to help heal our ailing cultures and this world."

—NINA SIMONS, cofounder of Bioneers

"In this moving spiritual memoir, Tull lifts up the role of darkness as teacher, healer, and guide, revealing spacious and emergent possibilities. Each chapter offers mindful inquiry and experiential practice gateways to explore the potential in darkness to restore inner strength and wholeness. Drawing on spiritual traditions from Zen to shamanism, Tull invites readers to engage the luminous capacities of darkness to counteract the overlighting of the planet and truly learn to see in the dark."

—STEPHANIE K̶ author of *Green Buddhism*

Luminous Darkness

AN ENGAGED BUDDHIST APPROACH
TO EMBRACING THE UNKNOWN

Deborah Eden Tull

SHAMBHALA

SHAMBHALA PUBLICATIONS, INC.
2129 13th Street
Boulder, Colorado 80302
www.shambhala.com

Permissions: Thomas Berry excerpt on p. 176 from *The Great Work* by Thomas Berry (Crown, 2000) courtesy of Penguin Random House LLC. Wendell Berry excerpt on p. 15 from Wendell Berry, "To Know the Dark" from *New Collected Poems*. Copyright © 1970, 2012 by Wendell Berry. Reprinted with the permission of The Permissions Company, LLC on behalf of Counterpoint Press, counterpointpress.com. Rainer Maria Rilke excerpt on p. 41 from "Du Dunkelheit, aus der . . . /You, darkness, of whom . . ." by Rainer Maria Rilke, *Rilke's Book of Hours: Love Poems to God* by Rainer Maria Rilke, translated by Anita Barrows and Joanna Macy, translation copyright © 1996 by Anita Barrows and Joanna Macy. Used by permission of Riverhead, an imprint of Penguin Publishing Group, a division of Penguin Random House LLC. All rights reserved.

COVER ART: © Jasmine Co
COVER DESIGN: Katrina Noble
INTERIOR DESIGN: Katrina Noble

9 8 7 6 5 4 3 2 1

First Edition
Printed in the United States of America
Shambhala Publications makes every effort to print on acid-free, recycled paper.
Shambhala Publications is distributed worldwide by Penguin Random House, Inc., and its subsidiaries.

LIBRARY OF CONGRESS CATALOGING-IN-PUBLICATION DATA
Names: Tull, Deborah Eden, author.
Title: Luminous darkness: an engaged Buddhist approach to embracing the unknown / Deborah Eden Tull.
Description: Boulder, Colorado: Shambhala, [2022] | Includes bibliographical references.
Identifiers: LCCN 2021056017 | ISBN 9781645470779 (trade paperback)
Subjects: LCSH: Meditation. | Light and darkness. | Light and Darkness—Psychological aspects. | Light and darkness—Philosophy.
Classification: LCC BL627 .T848 2022 | DDC 158.1/2—dc23/eng/20220103
LC record available at https://lccn.loc.gov/2021056017

DEDICATION

Light does not come from light, but from darkness.

MIRCEA ELIADE, *The Sacred and The Profane*

Much of my life has been an exploration of what makes a good teacher. I dedicate this book to the beloved memory of Walter Makichen, compassionate guide, mystic, friend, and one who walked between the worlds in devoted service and dynamic amusement. . . . And to Ramada for helping me to see through the embers and ashes of who I thought I was in order to know my true nature.

I also dedicate this book to Bobby (Robert Anderson), whose radiant beauty emanated even from the harsh confines of prison walls—and whose tragic story is shared by far too many extraordinary humans due to the brutality of systemic racism and the criminal justice system within the United States.

Lastly, I dedicate this book to my ancestors—dharmic and karmic— who revered the night sky and who protected the earth's endarkened sanctuaries for restoration, communion, and vision.

CONTENTS

ACKNOWLEDGMENTS

Long ago, a beloved teacher encouraged me to say yes to those projects, which both serve our world and command me to meet my next growth edge. This book has been one of these divine assignments.

I wrote *Luminous Darkness* backward into the present, allowing this book to reveal itself to me. This is how we walk through life—backward into the dark. Into the unknown. We lean into the support of those already behind us. And I felt the support and loving companionship of so many from throughout my life during this journey into endarkenment.

It is a privilege to be awake to the hidden dimensions or magic that make up the creative process. I acknowledge with love and gratitude the myriad invisible processes that went into creating this book. I drank from many wisdom streams and birthed this book through remarkable conversations. My writing called into play the synergy of dark and light, through meditation, journeying, dreaming, poetry, and subconscious churnings alongside compassionate discipline, perseverance, research, editing, and organized effort.

Boundless gratitude to Mark D'Aquila, my husband, playmate, partner in service, and the love of my life! Your support, companionship, sense of humor, and patience nourished me day and night throughout the writing of this book.

Thank you to my mom, Tanya Tull, a force of nature and lifelong inspiration whose hidden superpower is editing. And to my entire family who are always there supporting me. You know who you are.

Thank you to Coleen O'Shea for empowering my vision, and to the entire Shambhala team—Beth Frankl and Breanna Locke, and freelancers

Jill Rogers and Sylveon Consulting—for helping to bring this project to graceful completion. I am grateful for the brilliant creative support I received from Susanna Stromberg, Sharon Zetter, Jane Gould, Jasmine Co for her incredible artwork, and many others.

I am ever grateful for inspiring conversations and experiences shared with Joanna Macy, Claire Wings, Simon Buxton, Pam Weiss, Ruth King, Andrew Holecek, Lazlo Paule, Nina Simons, and other extraordinary beings for deepening my understanding and embodiment.

I cherish my kinship with the Fierce Compassion Sangha, the Mindful Living Revolution board and community, all participants in my Heart of Listening and Seeing with the Heart trainings, our monthly Women's group, and all who dive deeply into practice with me.

Lastly, I bow deeply, in boundless reverence, to the land I inhabit. And to the night skies for inviting me into cocreative relationship and continually reminding me of my place here.

INTRODUCTION

How I Fell in Love with the Dark

In the fall of 2018, I stood under the night sky in Big Sur, at the mystical crossroads of forest and ocean. It was midnight. The sky was the pitch-black canvas for an explosion of stars, and I was encircled by cool crisp ocean air. Resting in open awareness, in suspended fascination with the infinite vastness of the sky around me, I had an unusual encounter. I felt the subtle but certain presence of two stars connecting with me in the darkness of the night. While I had decades of experience in engaged meditation and earth-based practices that had included subtle and profound communication with the spirits that animate our planet, I had never had nor imagined such an experience with stars. While I had often enjoyed the ritual of meditating outside at night, my fixed sense of self dissolving beneath the immensity of the Milky Way, my experience on this unique night surprised me. It felt at once perfectly ordinary and extraordinary to become intuitively aware of two stars that seemed to be actively communicating with me.

The veil between the worlds disappeared as I began receiving quiet instruction and transmission about darkness and its teachings. It was the kind of communication that was nonverbal, received instead through image, metaphor, and feeling. It enlivened me, and I felt the steadfast embrace of communion.

I woke up the next morning somehow altered by the encounter and by the period of deep contemplation that followed. Over a number of weeks, I continued to feel my attention directed and redirected in awe toward the darkness of the night skies. Sitting in meditation during the day or lying down to rest at night, I would find myself again experiencing a fertile cocoon of other-worldly transmission. Although I was aware of ancient civilizations that had profound relationships with darkness, the night sky, and the stars, this was counterintuitive to the culture in which I had been raised. In the brightly lit modern world, physical darkness is considered more of an inconvenience than an ally. In a state of receptive listening, I felt the divine darkness showing me something more, something I had always known.

Though meditation does not teach us to fetishize mystical experience, the path of *waking up* reminds us that the human realm is not the only realm. Meditation teaches us to live in a state of openness and deep listening—not only in relation to humanity but in relationship with the cosmos. By engaging in *embodied listening* as a way of life, we remember ourselves as part of the interdependent nexus of nature's intelligence.

I never expected to write a book about darkness. As soon as the idea took root, however, the profound relevance of this topic for today's world, for meditators, and perhaps for every spiritual pathway became clear. Although darkness—both physical and metaphorical—is today a widely misunderstood aspect of nature, its restorative medicine was cherished by our ancestors and many ancient civilizations across the world's continents.

The value of darkness is unmistakable when we observe the natural world. Rediscovering darkness and thus reuniting dark and light, yin and yang, the receptive and active aspects of nature, is nourishment that each and every one of us needs in order to be whole. Throughout history, humans across the world have sought out physical darkness as a spiritual guide, ally, and source of restoration. We have communed with one another under the midnight skies. We have valued time spent in caves and caverns. The seeds that sustain us have forever germinated in the earth's darkened topsoil, and our existence depends upon the pollination performed by honeybees who inhabit dark hives. We have sought guidance through nocturnal dreams for thousands of years. Today, darkness retreats are still practiced within the

Tibetan Dzogchen teachings, European shamanism, Taoism, Christianity, and other spiritual traditions. But in the modern world, we spend very little time in physical darkness except when we sleep.

I see a connection between the overlighting of our planet and the overlighting of human consciousness. The dominant paradigm has become focused on the rational mind, linear thought, and hierarchical perception, as well as on activity and productivity. This book offers a restorative alternative.

The global challenges we face today provide an unprecedented invitation for collective transformation. There is an opportunity to remember how to listen, see, and sense clearly from the heart. There are hidden powers within us that we have forgotten that await us in the presence of darkness. True vision is received through learning to see in the dark. I believe that what we need today is *visionary activism*.

Humans have been conditioned to fear that which we do not know, that which we cannot see or understand. It is true that sometimes the dark—both physical and symbolic—can seem threatening. I will offer guidance in this book for working with that fear. Rather than turn away, I encourage you to consider the fear we might experience beneath the new moon, which simultaneously casts upon us the darkest sky and the most expansive and thrilling view of the universe, or the fear we feel in a moment of vulnerability in which we are seen and met with compassion in the very place we have held or hidden shame. Consider the fear we experience during the creative process in which new possibility bursts through the void as we take a bold risk in our artistic imagination. Or the fear we might feel when a lover we trust invites us outside of our comfort zone, revealing hidden chambers we have shied away from, renewing vitality that had been buried in the trenches of habit.

Two months before my experience in Big Sur, I had had another profound experience on the final evening session of a silent meditation retreat that I led at Land of Medicine Buddha in Northern California. It was then that the seed of this book was planted. In a candlelit meditation hall, surrounded by majestic redwood trees, I invited questions about integrating the practices we had engaged in. The room felt still, settled, and tender. A young student asked me, "What advice do you have for the younger generations, given the state of the world we are inheriting?" I held the question in quietude for a moment, sensing my own mix of feelings for all those who have inherited even more challenges than my own generation. I felt everyone in the room, regardless of age, sync into resonance with sobering collective grief about the state of our world. "For every human being alive at this time, I believe it is time to let go of our current obsession with enlightenment and include the teachings of endarkenment. That is, it is time to commit to turning *toward* rather than *away from* darkness and to learn to perceive with the heart—beyond unconscious bias and hierarchical perception. I believe that darkness—physical and symbolic— is deeply misunderstood, yet it offers powerful medicine for the times we face and our relationships with ourselves, one another, and our planet."

As the conversation continued, I realized something I'd long been aware of but never fully or publicly acknowledged: *Darkness has been my greatest teacher.* Mine has been a path, not of seeking illumination or transcendence but of finding wholeness through surrendering to the fertile and dark emptiness from which revelation arises. Mine has been a dharma path of endarkenment and of helping myself and others to reawaken to the teachings of darkness.

As a female dharma teacher who has navigated chronic and debilitating illness, been engaged in the heartbreak of environmental and social justice work for many years, and experienced the liminal space between the worlds throughout my lifetime, darkness has offered medicine, serenity, strength, and healing. It has taken me time, however, to realize the value of endarkenment alongside enlightenment, in a world where there is a preference for light over dark and where illumination is not only celebrated but the "goal" of spiritual practice. Darkness has been my guide in embodying relational intelligence, partnership with nature, and a joie de vivre that cannot be accessed when we look only toward the light.

Enlightenment Is Neither an End nor a Goal

Teachings on enlightenment saved my life. Buddhist meditation and enlightenment teachings offered a path for going beyond suffering and dissolving my fixed sense of self, in order to reawaken to who and what I actually was. While it was hardly what I expected, meditation also revealed for me the degree to which human consciousness has been impacted by generations of patriarchy, anthropocentrism, colonialism, capitalism, individualism, and consumerism.

Hierarchical perception is the root of delusion beneath every *ism* we face as a species today. It impacts some of us much more harshly and directly than others; however, it impacts each and every one of us in some way, regardless of gender, belief system, ethnicity, or race. Hierarchy assumes superiority and inferiority. I write this book with the hope that humanity can address the seed from which it evolves, as well as the fruit that it propagates.

Meditation practice revealed the ways in which I had inherited the trance of hierarchical perception. The world I grew up in celebrated the exclusive value of light, action, speed, productivity, attainment, destination, linear time, rationality, and logic. Meditation gradually reawakened me to the balance that bridges the power of dark and light, yin and yang, and deep feminine and sacred masculine, the receptive and expressive aspects of our nature.

One of my purposes in writing this book is to address *spiritual bypassing*. Spiritual bypassing is the use of spiritual practices and concepts to avoid and even deny painful realities throughout our human experience. This perpetuates reality avoidance, "feel good" escapism, and the use of spirituality to find an island of peace to hold on to. There is no island of peace. There is no escape from the mess of our heartbroken world. Only when we stop trying to escape, and invite the whole messy world into our hearts, will our heartbreak be made whole. This requires us to become uncompromisingly real and remember, instead, the loving embrace that leaves nothing out.

Spiritual practice is as prone to unconscious bias and limiting assumptions as any other domain of human experience. Contemporary spiritual teachings often encourage an "up, up, and away" approach to awakening, taking people "out of their bodies" and promoting transcendence, elevation, philosophizing, and attainment. There can be a conscious or unconscious assumption that enlightenment is an end and a goal when it is neither. In the pursuit of enlightenment, I have often witnessed meditators striving to "get to the light" with the assumption that spiritual light is the product of spiritual practice. This feeds a duality that is fundamentally not helpful between body/spirit, sky/earth, good/bad, subject/object, and consciousness/unconsciousness.

I have witnessed people discount the body, human emotions, shadow, the subconscious, and the great mystery itself. Our *shadows* are those attributes and qualities that are inconsistent with the self-concept we are trying to maintain but that we are often unaware of. This has resulted in entrenched fear and discomfort binding many generations.

The bias toward light over dark caused tremendous confusion in my own early path as a meditator. I am grateful that, over time, practice has led me to clear up major misconceptions around spirituality and to help others do the same. My path has been about learning to stay present to the wordless invisible mystery, not knowing, and the deeper darker undercurrents of life, moment by moment. It has been about coming home to the immeasurable wisdom of my body. It has been about surrendering the comforts of the logical and linear mind and welcoming other forms of knowing, which affirm my place in the intricate web of interdependence.

Spiritual practice is a process of finding freedom by turning toward and letting go of fear. Turning toward is the motion that allows us to remember the compassion that is who we really are. If we fear darkness and the great void, then how can we awaken?

This book is an invitation to remember what one half of your nature cannot access alone. This book beckons you to get to know the friend, teacher, sanctuary, and consciousness of darkness. It is only when we allow ourselves, repeatedly, to commune with the elemental darkness that we gradually open to an unwavering inner light regardless of our outer condition. Dark and light work in a reciprocal relationship to affirm true nature. In this age of disruption and anxiety about the future of our planet, the divine darkness may be our greatest ally rather than a danger to be feared.

Many of you reading this book have experienced the creative tension that exists between feeling grief for our planet and its people and species and feeling a passionate responsibility to respond. Our world is facing unprecedented challenges, yet many of you sense that we were made for this time. As we turn toward rather than away from our pain for our world, we realize a deeper sense of purpose. When we remember that we are in this together, we expand our capacity to love across lines. When we *feel and sense*, rather than try to *think* our way through it, we access the wisdom of our natural feedback systems as members of planet Earth. And the more we learn to include the invisible along with the visible world in our awareness, the more we gain access to a hidden source of energy with which to meet—with love—the myriad challenges that we face today.

In this book, I will suggest ways that the divorce of dark from light has impacted humanity spiritually, psychologically, emotionally, ecologically, interpersonally, and globally. I believe it has perpetuated fear of the unknown. It has perpetuated a pattern of reactivity and divisiveness in which we perceive anything different as "other." It has contributed to systemic racism and discrimination against people with darker skin, as well as misogyny and transphobia. It has contributed to the excessive artificial lighting of our planet, climate change, species extinction, and human domination over the natural world. It has fed disrespect for the slow and invisible processes of nature and consciousness.

Before We Go Deeper . . .

The English language is very limited when it comes to spirituality, consciousness, and mysticism. Humanity's long legacy of spiritual language has been replaced primarily with marketplace language. We will explore marketplace mentality later in this book. I have done my best to find language that is accessible, meaningful, and unbiased. I acknowledge, however, that all of the English language carries some cultural bias and binary tendency. I offer basic definitions as we go to create the context for this book and to help clarify your understanding of the terms used.

I am a white, middle-class woman who understands that the very opportunity I have had to steep myself in formal spiritual practice in this lifetime is a result of privilege. Buddhism teaches that being human is all that's required to awaken. Unfortunately, in the Western world today, the leisure to engage in formal spiritual practice has become a privilege of money and time. It is vital to recognize the challenges and barriers to formal spiritual practice presented by socioeconomic disparities in our society. The day-to-day struggle to maintain a mortgage, pay rent, or combat food insecurity can be seen most clearly through the lens of systemic racism. Black people and people of color face these struggles dramatically disproportionately to whites within the United States. To create a more equitable and just society within a context of generational and systemic racism requires recognition of the social, economic, and racial inequities that currently exist. It also requires innovative and concerted strategies to overcome them. Most racial justice activists would argue that there are many other necessary and vital things that we must fight for besides meeting basic needs, such as protection of social and political rights, as well as protection of racial identity and experiences.

My intention has been to maintain awareness of the complexities of being a white woman writing a book that speaks to the crisis of our times. I sense, humbly, that I will be learning in this domain for the rest of my life. I can only speak from the specificity of my own experience, as it might resonate with certain universal truths that people from diverse backgrounds share.

While my practice has been anchored in Zen Buddhism, my spiritual path has been generously unconventional. My teachings have been

informed by decades of Buddhist practice, European shamanism and animism, deep ecology, social justice, environmental work, conscious dance,
and the essential wisdom of nature. I believe that nature is our greatest
teacher and that we can only realize teachings through direct experience,
through our bodies rather than concepts. The diverse traditions I speak
from share a commitment to liberation through direct experience.

Some recommendations for reading this book include the following:

- **Go slowly.** Slowing down is one of the basic teachings of endarkenment. Rather than hurry through the chapters of this book, please
  allow yourself to slow down in order to sense and feel your way
  through this journey. At the end of every chapter, I offer "mindful
  inquiry" exercises to help you integrate these teachings into your own
  life's experience. Mindful inquiry is the practice of holding a question in your present-moment awareness and allowing for insight and
  understanding to unfold organically. You are invited to pick one or
  more questions to work with in each chapter. You can go as deeply or
  as gently as you choose, depending on your history and how supported you feel at this time.

  As you reflect on the mindful inquiry questions I offer, there is no
  need to strive to find an answer. Rather than try to analyze or figure
  out the answer, simply listen within and stay as present as you can
  to what is happening in your body-heart-mind. Notice what feelings
  and reflections might emerge from the spaciousness with which you
  listen. Feel free to keep a journal for recording your awarenesses
  through writing or drawing.

- **Invoke beginner's mind.** No matter where you are on your spiritual
  journey, whether you are new to practice or have been meditating for
  decades, whether you are on a spiritual or secular path, a religious
  practitioner or a skeptic, I encourage you to read this book with a
  beginner's mind. Let yourself be open and curious and available for
  a fresh and evolving perspective. Do not believe what I say; rather,

look within to see how what I'm suggesting resonates with your experience of being human. At the foundation of endarkenment is an invitation to reclaim one's internal authority instead of assuming that the authority is "out there."

If there are teachings or concepts that you find difficult to understand, please be patient with yourself. The wisdom of endarkenment is so contrary to the dominant paradigm that you might not have a reference point for some of these teachings—even if you have a long-term meditation or spiritual practice. Please do the practices offered in this book and let your experience inform your understanding. Spiritual realization occurs on three levels: understanding, practice, and embodied realization. There is no need or way to rush this process. The process itself, unique for each one of us, is the awakening. Some of the exercises are *relational mindfulness* practices that you can do with a partner. For a more in-depth exploration of relational mindfulness, please refer to my book *Relational Mindfulness: A Handbook for Deepening Our Connection with Ourselves, Each Other, and Our Planet.*

- **Be mindful of duality.** In this book I will at times discuss the specific qualities of light and dark. Darkness has luminous gems to offer us and has been overlooked. At the same time, I am inviting you to move beyond the duality of light and dark. These intentions are not in opposition to each other. When we move out of duality, we do not eliminate the two qualities or objects that occupy the poles of this duality. They are part of the full spectrum.

- **Practice nonjudgment and self-compassion.** You will be invited to identify and release limiting beliefs that you may have held or participated in for a long time, as you read this book. You may uncover dusty cobwebby belief systems that have taken up space in your subconscious for decades or the span of your entire lifetime. Please practice nonjudgment. Be kind and gentle with yourself. Allow yourself to feel fully whatever feelings arise. If resistance emerges, my encouragement is to notice your resistance without judging it or taking it personally. In other words, there is no need to resist resistance.

Likewise, it is never helpful to create a standard out of spiritual teachings. It does not serve to judge yourself or others for thinking/speaking from the hierarchical perception this book brings awareness to. The opportunity is to see ourselves and one another from the heart.

If the topic of darkness triggers difficult emotions from your past or present—when you might have felt that it was just *too dark*—please remember that you are not alone. Many of us, including me, have been there too. It is important to tether ourselves to steadfast support through those experiences. There will be practices where I invite you to close your eyes for an extended period of time or engage in a nocturnal meditation. If any of these practices feel triggering, there is no need to engage in them. Consider modifying the practice or simply continue to the next section.

I share these teachings in loving-kindness to all beings, visible and invisible, seen and unseen, born and unborn, spanning deep time and space. I hope that this book offers timeless wisdom and support for transforming consciousness as we navigate our changing planet. In the spirit of humility and courage, I acknowledge that the questions I ask us to explore in this book are questions that we can only answer together.

PART ONE

The Journey into Endarkenment

This part invites us into the spirit of possibility. We will explore the role of darkness within the natural world and the overlighting of our planet, which has taken place dramatically in the past fifty years. We will explore some of our associations with the dark and open our minds to redefining darkness and endarkenment. We will turn within to connect with the divine darkness.

1

Redefining Darkness

The Physical and Symbolic Invitations of Darkness

> To go in the dark with a light is to know the light.
> To know the dark, go dark. Go without sight,
> and find that the dark, too, blooms and sings,
> and is traveled by dark feet and dark wings.
>
> WENDELL BERRY[1]

I LIVE IN THE LUSH, dense, dark, temperate rainforest of Western North Carolina. In the spring and summer, when the mountains explode with the green of trees, ferns, herbs, fungi, and flowers, my husband and I enjoy exploring the deep off-trail woods. There is no known direction as we walk. No set human-created path to follow. We let our intuitions guide us, or we find a meandering creek to lead the way. The forest is wildly dynamic, pregnant with life, and we walk, barefoot, among leaves, pine needles, rocks, earth, and wet marsh. We move slowly and with care, guided by curiosity, wonder, and body awareness. The terrain is a balance of nocturnal shade contrasted with patches of golden sunlight bursting with photosynthesis. The forest expresses nature's stillness and complexity, harmony and chaos, in perfect balance. Linear time dissolves as we then rest for what seems like hours under the sheltering shade of the trees.

Walking off-trail through a dense forest is the metaphor I will use for our journey into endarkenment. There is no existing human-made trail for understanding darkness. A brightly lit path with signs pointing out the direction will never allow us to sense and feel our way into the mystery itself. Additionally, everyone's journey will be different and unique.

The forest wilderness is a metaphor for both the spiritual journey and our collective journey through today's global uncertainty. We can no longer rely on our existing orientation to guide us. The challenges we face call for the development of new relational forms of knowing and navigation. The forms we seek, however, already exist within each of us.

Like a thicketed forest, the terrain of darkness can only be traversed by sensing, feeling, inquiring, and listening with our whole bodies, being both curious and humble at the same time. A dissertation that "sheds light" on darkness would merely offer a path into the light or the known. The creative challenge for me as a dharma teacher and writer is to invite you into an embodied exploration.

For those of you who are wondering, *What is endarkenment? What exactly do you mean by darkness?* I will soon offer definitions and propose fresh ways of perceiving darkness. By so doing, I will encourage the spirit of possibility rather than conclusion.

The architecture of this book will invite you to question your existing associations with darkness—both physical and metaphorical. We will explore some of the emotional, psychological, spiritual, and ecological repercussions of rejecting darkness. We will then invoke the spiritual teachings revealed by divine darkness, ultimately embracing an expansively larger perspective where dark and light exist in partnership within ourselves and our world. Finally, I will explore the inspiring invitation that endarkenment offers as we face unprecedented global change. I encourage you to let each chapter open your perception to different and fresh dimensions of what darkness is.

The first step to understanding endarkenment is to become curious about darkness beyond your familiar associations. Be open to what you don't know that you don't know . . . about darkness and light, about yourself, about the mystery itself. We can learn to meet the unknown and the experience of not knowing with an open and humble heart, much more full of wonder and willingness than fear. Endarkenment celebrates five aspects of embodied meditation and spirituality:

1. **Our awakening through embodiment and earth connection.** Only by bringing our awareness down into our bodies and affirming our connection with the earth, away from the realm of concepts and ideas, do we remember who we really are.

2. **The restoration of our ability to see clearly with the heart by surrendering to receptivity and by taking responsibility for the lens through which we are perceiving.** I am not referring solely to the organ of the heart, though it's an extraordinary organ of relational intelligence. I am speaking of the heart of our beings, the sacred integration of body-heart-mind accessed through meditation.

3. **The reclamation of our true nature or original consciousness by releasing hierarchical perception.** All hierarchical thinking is a distortion in consciousness, as I will explore in this book. There is no exception. Hierarchy was invented by humankind, and it has been passed down through the generations.

4. **The deepening of our relationship with ourselves and others and our intercommunicative relationship with nature, the visible and invisible matrix of life.** Endarkenment invites us into multinatural awareness, interbeing through pathways for communication and collaboration with life. These pathways already exist within our bodies. While earth-based and animistic traditions have celebrated multinatural awareness throughout history, contemporary

society is limited by a human-centered and technology-centered paradigm.

5. **The willingness to meet all life—including shadows—with fierce compassion.** Embodied meditation embraces all aspects of our humanity, rather than trying to transcend dark to get to the light.

*   *   *

EXPERIENTIAL PRACTICE: MEETING DARKNESS

Please prepare to pause and close your eyes for a few minutes. Set the intention, with eyes closed, to take in a few deep, conscious breaths. Feel the air as it enters your body, fills your body, and leaves your body. Be aware of your body's connection to gravity and sense the earth beneath you. Once you have settled into darkened stillness, notice with curiosity what is moving through your internal landscape. Go slowly . . . noticing your body, mind, and feelings.

When you are ready, keep your eyes closed and become aware of the outer landscape of sound, temperature, and the way the space you are in feels.

Then, continue to remain in the darkened stillness and allow yourself to become aware of the inner and outer landscapes at the same time.

Notice how, void of visual perception, all of your other senses awaken. In the darkness, our perception opens beyond our habitual visual orientation to life.

The Unique Invitation of Endarkenment

We are not an individual. We are a vast network of molecules, energies, vibrations, the interconnectedness of being is who we are.

PAUL STAMETS[2]

A forest is, above all else, a community of living beings. When we walk mindfully through a forest community, we become one with the trees, mycelia, lichens, birds, and myriad forms of visible and invisible life that exist in constant collaboration. We learn, through meditation, to perceive the unique tree and the forest at the same time, with the backdrop of interdependence as our foundation. Just like traversing a thicketed forest, beyond the familiarity of visual and rational perception, fluorescent lights and computer screens, endarkenment invites us to access a deeper source of knowledge. We might think of this as embodied and relational intelligence rather than intellect-based forms of knowing.

One of the lessons I learned in the years I spent living in silence as a Zen Buddhist monk and the years I spent stewarding land as an organic farmer is that the natural world is constantly communicating with us. It is always inviting us into collaboration, speaking to us and through us, if we are willing to listen.

Awakening is about remembering ourselves as part of the living web of interconnection—not conceptually, but experientially. Endarkenment invites us down into our bodies to access the spiritual qualities of receptivity, curiosity, attunement, stillness, surrender, deep listening, slowing down, and not knowing. We will not be able to allow the ego to dissolve if we insist on identifying with its limited perception. We are not separate from other humans or the plants, flowers, minerals, fungi, insects, and creatures visible and invisible of our universe.

While the modus operandi of the modern world is one of speed, global uncertainty requires us to slow down so we can ask fresh questions. In the rubble of the narratives that are clearly no longer working for humanity, we are rediscovering seeds of possibility. By excavating human consciousness, we are remembering simple truths we have forgotten. Many of these truths are hidden in darkness, like the luminous pearl within the dark shell of the oyster.

In the darkness, which does not discriminate, we are relieved of the confines of ego to remember something much greater to which we all belong. Darkness is the field of freedom beyond duality. We experience the restorative aspect of nature that is necessary to sustain and regenerate all of life. We let go of our familiar script to meet the moment as an empty canvas or vessel, open to possibility and connection.

Endarkenment begins by redefining discomfort, uncertainty, and perceived obstacles not as challenges but as invitations, not as signs of things to turn away from but instead as welcoming thresholds to move directly toward. I offer my own story of endarkenment, which will weave through these chapters and their teachings, with the hope that it can touch your path more directly.

Examining Unconscious Biases

To begin our journey together, I invite you to ask yourself, *What are my current associations with darkness?* For instance, you might associate darkness with discomfort, sadness, evil, secrecy, danger, lack of clarity, malicious intent, or the unknown. Then there's also darkness in the environment (dark night, dark clouds, dark sky), darkness as it refers to physical coloring (dark hair, dark skin, dark eyes), and darkness in the human psyche (dark emotions, dark human shadows, dark night of the soul).

What strikes me is that most of our associations point to darkness as negative. Sinister. Scary. Ominous. Undesirable. Dangerous. Unsafe. We've come to associate darkness with much of what we reject as a collective. We prefer light and associate it with not only daytime and summer but also positivity, play, rightness, safety, ease, purity, clarity, spirituality, achievement, and all things good. In fact, we usually perceive darkness as the absence of light. I have always found this interesting because we do not generally perceive light as the absence of dark. We put light on an unquestioned pedestal above dark.

We oddly label challenging times, difficult people, and this age of global uncertainty as "dark times." Historically, the Middle Ages, or medieval period, are known as the Dark Ages and are perceived as a primitive, unsophisticated, crass, immoral, and even sinister period in human history.[3] Originally, however, the word *dark* was used to describe the medieval period only because historians had very little access to information about it. The term *dark* originally meant "not much known."

We use the phrases *dark matter*[4] and *dark energy* to refer to more than 95 percent of the energy density in the universe, which has never been directly detected in the laboratory. Roughly 95 percent of the universe remains a complete mystery to science. In other words, scientific research has found that only 4.6 percent of life as we know it, including the Earth, planets, and stars, is made up of atomic matter. Because we have no idea what the roughly remaining 95 percent is, we refer to it as "dark."

While our negative associations with darkness might seem innocent, I believe there are profound implications in our historical and collective rejection of darkness. The continual reference to darkness as negative and sinister—and the assumed divide between light and dark—has created a severe tear in the fabric of human relationship. It has caused a dualistic fracture in how we see everything—good/bad, right/wrong, higher/lower, worthy/unworthy.

These dualistic associations have contributed to systemic racism, classism, misogyny, sexism, domination over nature, and the demonization of mental illness and physical disability. They also create an obstacle to knowing our inner truth, which in its full form expresses the radiance of both light and dark.

It can be difficult to understand how strongly historical trauma has impacted human consciousness without acknowledging the *intersubjective nature of conditioning*. What this means is that people tend not to question thought patterns that are shared by friends, neighbors, relatives, and leaders even when they might be untrue. We are like fish that cannot always see the water in which they swim. They continue to take in water through their gills even though the water itself is unwholesome and unclean. Over time this effort becomes exhausting and unsustainable. While it is the imperative of the human heart to move beyond the comforts, restrictions, and boundaries of conditioned thought, the intersubjective nature of conditioning causes us to accept things that are not real as true and absolute—we cannot see how murky the water really is, so we do nothing to change it. Nature models light and dark as equally valuable, sacred partners in the sustenance of life on earth. This is why I believe that we need endarkenment alongside enlightenment. In a world where so many people today are struggling to integrate the increasingly complex state of the world they have inherited into their psyche, I have seen people assume that what they perceive as darkness within themselves equates to failure and thus try to hide it.

From working with thousands of people over the past twenty-five years, I have observed a tendency toward ignoring or negating a vital part of being human, which is to feel fully. To do so requires embracing our sensitivity and vulnerability. With so many people looking toward the external world or rationalization for answers, the deeper knowing that comes from being present with the mystery itself can be overlooked. I wonder if we are shielding ourselves from life itself; turning away from one half of being human—the receptive aspect of our nature—in pursuit of the technological and linear vision of "human progress."

Many systems humans have relied upon for generations in the age of Industrial Capitalism have failed us. At the same time, the acceleration of climate change and the ensuing loss of living systems on our planet has caused upheaval in what once felt like solid ground. We have collectively left the familiar shore and cannot yet see the shore where we will land. When we allow ourselves to stay present through the unknown, we access a compass far more multidimensional than our linear mind. When we face the depth of our collective suffering with willingness and patience, buoyancy replaces the fear that we will drown. It is in the deepest darkest caverns that our spiritual light is unleashed, and we trust that this light is shared by all of humanity. It is, in fact, our true nature and who we really are as a collective.

The Divine Darkness Revealed

Every day, priests minutely examine the dharma
And endlessly chant complicated sutras.
Before doing that, though, they should learn

How to read the love letters sent by the wind and rain,

the snow and moon.

IKKYU SOJUN[5]

I have found darkness to be so multidimensional and rich that a simple definition can barely touch on it. It is like resting in fascination with a shaded patch of earth in a dynamic forest, being mind-blown by how many microclimates exist within nature's womb. In other words, darkness—literal and symbolic—has myriad teachings to offer us. It offers personal, interpersonal, transpersonal, and societal medicine for our world, and we will explore all of these through the chapters of this book.

If we look and listen more deeply to what darkness actually is—literally and metaphorically—we will recognize it as a treasure and boundless source of collective medicine. While countless ancient traditions have celebrated darkness as a living spirit or consciousness, modern Western civilization has failed to recognize its innate value.

All of life arises from darkness, including insight. In meditation practice, we encounter darkness as the void or the field of groundlessness. We also speak about this as emptiness, spaciousness, and the boundless nature of awareness.

Darkness, as an element of nature, carries qualities that are receptive, or yin, like stillness, quietude, and rest, while bright illumination conveys qualities that are active, or yang, such as motion, animation, and productivity. Think of how you feel when you are resting in the shade of a tree, gazing at the night sky, or relaxing in *shavasana*.

Darkness as a metaphor points to the unseen, the invisible and unknown rather than to the visible and known. We might say that darkness is stored energy and limitless possibility rather than that which has already been realized or expressed.

In meditation, we enter deep states of receptivity or darkness, through which we also access light. We practice resting in the deeper recesses of human consciousness. We surrender to darkness by letting go of labeling and trying to make order out of life. Not limited by our visual perception, we access the original consciousness or awareness that welcomes everything. We learn, through meditation, that those experiences—which appear to us as the absence of light—can be gateways to expanding consciousness.

In Buddhism, enlightenment points to awakening and the end of suffering. Enlightenment was also, however, a philosophical movement in the eighteenth century that reflected traditional religious, political, and social ideas emphasizing rationalism, cognitive understanding, and spiritual attainment.

The idea of enlightenment has been filtered through many generations of patriarchy, colonialism, capitalism, imperialism, and individualism— movements that continually discounted the physical body, human emotion, other forms of knowing, relationships, the natural world, feminine wisdom, indigenous spirituality, and the mystery itself. Enlightenment was also impacted by the European era between 952–1138 C.E., which, as documented in the film *The Burning Times*,[6] was when an estimated nine million people, primarily women, were killed in the persecution of witchcraft, paganism, and relational forms of knowledge. The Cartesian era, the Industrial Revolution, and the current technological revolution have also left their residue on enlightenment, and the modern-day meditation movement is not free from the residual biases of this history.

It is in our original nature to celebrate the spectrum and interplay of dark and light. Night and day, receptive and expressive, yin and yang, emptiness and fullness naturally exist in dynamic balance together. This can be difficult to grasp from binary perception, which continually insists on this *or* that instead of this *and* that. In order to know this balance, we need to remember how to respect darkness, listen to darkness, and, yes, to dance with darkness.

In the words of Eihei Dogen, the twelfth-century founder of Soto Zen, in "The Song of the Precious Mirror Samadhi":

Light and darkness are a pair, like the foot before

And the foot behind, in walking. Each thing has its own intrinsic
  value
And is related to everything else in function and position. [7]

When my husband and I take walks through the darkened off-trail woods, I always experience renewal at a far greater level than I expect. When we bathe in the forest's eternal moonlight, in the mix of life, death, decay, and regeneration, we let nature guide us. I feel invigorated by the emergent discovery that comes from not knowing where we are headed or what we will find. We get out of our heads, and our creative response quickens and becomes more refined. Some parts of the walk are easy and some involve getting mucky and muddy or meeting fear as we scale higher up. This keeps us awake to our physical senses and requires attunement within and without. My hope is that we can take an emergent walk in the divine dark together, listening to what is within and around us and being guided to a deeper understanding of who we are and what is possible for humanity.

*   *   *

MINDFUL INQUIRY

What were you taught about darkness, physical and symbolic, in the culture you grew up in? What assumptions and associations have you held personally about the dark that have come from conditioning you received from religion, culture, media, or family? And what has been the impact of this bias—on your relationship with yourself, with others, or with life itself?

In chapter 1, we explored the metaphor of walking off-trail through a dense forest. I spoke of the quality of mindful awareness that opens our subtle attunement to the world around us. In what ways do you practice and celebrate subtle attunement within and with the world around you? Perhaps through your relationship with the natural world? Through meditation? In the garden you tend or through conscious parenting and raising kids?

In what ways might you distract or busy yourself from deeper attunement, perhaps through double- or multitasking or over-thinking and thus avoiding or missing the opportunity to listen more deeply to yourself and the world around you? How does it feel to acknowledge this?

*   *   *

EXPERIENTIAL PRACTICE: THE PRESENCE OF DARKNESS

Please find a comfortable position to spend fifteen minutes in the pitch dark, with your eyes gently open. If your physical space is not completely dark, you can try this practice with your eyes closed, wearing a blindfold. Take in a few deep breaths and notice how it feels to relax in the dark. As you rest, bring subtle awareness to the impact of darkness on your internal and sensory experience. As much as possible, be disinterested in the commentary in your head and notice what is happening in your body. Be curious about where your physical body ends and the space around you begins. Notice what is arising in your heart. Become aware of how darkness enables you to listen to the deeper undercurrents of your experience. Become aware of the qualities of darkness itself.

When you release thinking of darkness as "the absence of light," what is your experience of it? What is darkness the presence of? When you release thinking of emptiness as the absence of something, what is it the presence of? There is no need to find a label for this, but there may be words, phrases, metaphors, or images that arise.

After fifteen minutes, allow yourself to gently transition back to normal awareness. Please make any notes that you would like to make in your journal if you are keeping one. You spend time resting or sleeping in the dark in every twenty-four-hour period, but how often do you allow yourself to bring subtle awareness to the unique presence of darkness?

2

Befriending the Night

The Radiant Teachings of Darkness

Only he who does not comprehend the darkness fears the night.

CARL JUNG[1]

WHEN I ARRIVED AT THE MONASTERY so many years ago, I still considered darkness to be a little frightening and somehow lonely. I was twenty-six years old when I gave away my belongings, shaved my head, and committed to a rigorous, spiritual training for the next seven and a half years. Becoming a Buddhist monastic instead of doing what most of my friends were doing in their twenties—establishing careers, starting families, or following a conventionally accepted path—was not a casual decision. I had experienced something through meditation deep within that began to feel more important to me than anything else. Despite my dedication to the environmental activism work I was engaged in at the time, I felt the mystery quietly commanding me to go deeper within. Alongside fear about what I would be letting go of as I entered monastic life, there was a small seed of courage guiding me.

There have been two interwoven threads throughout my spiritual path—dharma and the natural world. Nature is our greatest teacher. As a young adult exploring alternatives to the overconsumptive city in which I had been raised, I found reenchantment by choosing to live closer to the earth, in sustainable communities. Putting my hands in the soil felt honest and useful, free of the assumption that the human-centered modern world was everything.

Becoming a Zen monk provided the framework for living in service to life and focused on what is of essence/essential. I learned to meditate formally at the same time that I learned the art of organic farming and permaculture design. Permaculture design is the practice of learning from the intelligence of natural systems—from the brilliance of trees and termites to mycelia, honeybees, and dandelion colonies—to design sustainable systems for humans to live regeneratively on our planet.

Meditation affirmed my connection with the earth and my trust in the intelligence of life itself, beyond the presumed cleverness of the human mind. There was a quality of simplicity to both Zen practice and sustainable farming that I had always longed for—which felt like drinking pure crystalline water from a wild spring. Living in a world of such complexity and being aware of the complicated nature of my own mind, this spring flowed from an ancient source and gradually helped me to distill my awareness to what mattered the most. What is true? What is of essence and what is not? While I later came to teach interconnected consciousness to people living in all contexts—urban, suburban, and even prison—nature as guide has remained the foundation of every teaching I have ever offered.

The monastery was set on 350 acres in the Sierra wilderness, with vast expanses of oaks and manzanitas, mountains and prairies. There were twenty of us living there at that time, and we grew much of our own food, built our own structures, baked our own bread, and lived in silence. We followed a disciplined Zen schedule of sitting and working meditation, with community dharma meetings three times per week and holy leisure or free time every Sunday afternoon.

I lived alone in a tiny wooden hermitage in the woods, along a winding dirt path, and a fifteen-minute walk from any other dwelling. The monastery was off the grid and powered by solar energy. Once the sun set, we had very limited access to light and were immersed in the thick darkness of the night. Every evening, I lit an oil lamp and kept my flashlight close to my bedside. Although I had lived off the grid prior to that, in the initially lonely context of monasticism, I felt that I had never seen a sky as pitch black and seemingly endless as the Sierra night. The dark enveloped me with strange sounds and mysterious creatures, yellow-eyed nocturnal animals and insects, and the felt presence of invisibles that represented the unknown and the beyond. As the sun went down each day, I felt myself entering a gradual drop into both the peaceful stillness and the unsettling whispers of the night.

During this period in my life, I was going through a personal transformation that was full of both discovery and terror. This included a subtle examination of my ego and an overhaul of my orientation to life. I might describe it as shedding the layers of conditioning I had received from culture, family, media, and society to remember my connection to source. I felt myself releasing limiting beliefs and imprints that I had carried with me from childhood, and at times I held tightly to them for fear of who I would be without their familiar script.

There was a subtle tension between my soul's hunger for growth and the part of me that feared the unknown, that perceived change as loss. So much of spiritual practice seemed to be about cultivating trust in the moment while taking the next step into the void. I felt myself simultaneously experiencing death, rebirth, and the liminal states in between. The long, solitary, and secluded nights, which felt both thrilling and overwhelming at times, were a symbol and portal for this journey.

The Sacred Pulse of Night and Day

I spent the first eighteen years of my life in the city of Los Angeles, a landscape that was so lit up at night that it was nearly impossible to see the stars. My family went on camping trips in the Sierras, and I spent summers in the Santa Monica Mountains at a camp that was my childhood dreamscape. Aside from these experiences, it was a rare treat to encounter a dark night. At summer camp, we would hike up to a hilltop plateau on which we could find the perfect resting nook, lie down on our backs, and take in the dazzling and breathtaking midnight sky. We would rest there, entranced in a state of wonder, for what seemed like hours. Time would stop as we allowed ourselves to be held in the enchantment of the night. Watching the stars was a coveted and magical reminder of our connection with a mystery so much larger than ourselves. As soon as I returned home, however, the night sky was again dim with the pale-yellow hue of artificial light and only an occasional star flickering through.

In my early twenties, I was privileged to spend a great deal of time camping in the wilderness, and I savored evenings around a bonfire with friends. We would pack up blankets and layers of warm clothing and trek through the forest at night to a moonlit field or meadow to exchange poetry, song, and story. The nightscape served as both a portal to a mythological time and a compelling backdrop for a quality of social connection beyond the light of the day.

The monastery in the Sierras was fully removed from society and city lights, so once again the night sky confirmed my tiny place in the vast universe. I was completely alone in the night, accompanied by only the spirit of darkness and my own thoughts. In the nocturnal darkness, there was nothing to do but be in open space. At first, I had to face my tendency to fill this empty space with thought, as in sitting meditation. I gradually began to let that go, however, and surrender to empty space. In the dark, the activity of the conscious mind was composted and what remained was a vast empty expanse for integration, regeneration, serenity, and other forms of knowing.

I became keenly aware of my dream activity and the gestation and deeper communication that seemed to occur in the solitude of the night.

Throughout this time, I was also an organic gardener in an intimate relationship with the land I stewarded. I was aware of the subtle movement and impact of sunlight and shade throughout the day and equally aware of the invaluable nourishment of nighttime and moonlight for the plants, seeds, and creatures of the garden I tended. I surrendered to a simple and regenerative lifestyle at the monastery, practicing Zen awareness from sunrise to dusk and dark. I opened to a more organic rhythm with my body and with the natural world, and the assumed line between day and night began to dissolve. The continuous cycle and flow of each dawn, day, dusk, and night and the circadian rhythms of my own earthly body became my teachers and guides.

Living off the grid, I would rise early and more often than not observe the transition from night to dawn, as well as the transitions of sunset and moonrise. These experiences of sunrise and sunset and the liminal states in between affirmed my understanding that life was always in flux.

Like the inflow and outflow of the breath in meditation teaches us, from the brightest day to the darkest night, from the fertility of spring to the fallow of winter, there is one continual cycle of life. Every ending is a beginning, and every beginning is an ending. Life is a constant transient cycle of creating and letting go, birth and death, emerging and dissolving, light and dark.

Nothing exists in initiation or completion. Everything is moving, cycling, and in a continuous state of sacred flux. Like the wintertime or the exhale, some moments in the process are about slowing down and emptying, and like the springtime or the inhale, some celebrate acceleration and creation. Even diurnal plants and animals remain in the process of growth at night; it is merely slowed down and hidden in the dark. Life does not stop when the sun goes down.

Through Zen practice, I became aware of the many assumptions and systemic biases lodged in my psyche about all of life. This included the assumption that day was more valuable than night. This included the assumption that dark and light, night and day, were separate. At the same time, I began to learn how to meet pleasant internal states and more tumultuous states with a quality of kind neutrality, understanding my experience as a spectrum that contained it all.

I found humor in the use of the English language to reference "the past day" instead of "the past cycle of day and night." While life is based on a twenty-four-hour cycle that includes both night and day, we traditionally refer to it as "sun to sun," thereby highlighting the day (light) rather than the night (dark). Because day is the domain of activity, productivity, and the conscious mind, it is generally considered to be more relevant than the night. It is the night, however, that provides us time for restoration, stillness, empty space, and freedom for the subconscious mind.

In learning to befriend physical darkness and those aspects of my psyche I had labeled dark, I became ever-curious about my conditioned association of darkness as a negative. I became curious about the connections between physical and symbolic darkness, our habit of hierarchical perception. I became curious about the consciousness of darkness itself.

Natural Processes Made Possible by Physical Darkness

If we were to acknowledge the multitude of natural processes that are dependent on pure darkness, we would be in absolute awe. The positive response of biological systems to the presence of darkness is undeniable. Physical darkness is an invaluable aspect of nature. Darkness serves as the seat of gestation—the process of life being carried in the womb between conception and birth. Darkness serves the process of decomposition in which bodies of living organisms can be broken down and recycled to feed new life again. Darkness creates the dormancy and hibernation needed by plants and animals in the wintertime. Darkness protects moisture from evaporation in arid landscapes.

Because human beings are diurnal and, let's be honest, a bit anthropocentric, it is understandable that we might consider daytime to be more meaningful for our lives than the night. Light is essential for so many biological activities, such as photosynthesis and sight. However, the presence of uninterrupted periods of darkness, as well as the alternation of light and dark, is just as vital to biology: Darkness impacts the metabolism and behavior of animals, plants, and microbes. Dozens of species of nocturnal animals exist on our planet, including felines, raccoons, opossums, bats, kangaroos, and beavers. There are myriad species of plants and flowers that bloom in the dark and thrive in the absence of light, such as evening primrose, night-blooming cacti, moonflowers, certain herbaceous perennials, and certain shrubs and trees. The value of dark spaces and microlandscapes such as the cave, the shady tree, or a rock in the desert is immeasurable and cannot be recreated by light.

Let's take a deeper look at some of the processes in nature supported by darkness. When someone becomes pregnant, the embryo rests in the dark of their womb for nine months of gestation. This time period is dependent on the protection of darkness and the absence of light.

The caterpillar wraps itself in a silky cocoon, and within the sheath of this protected darkness it begins to completely metamorphose. First it digests itself, releasing enzymes that dissolve all of its tissues, and then it grows the adult body of the butterfly. Only after this dramatic transformation does it emerge again into the light.

In subterranean caves and gardens, crystals supported by the absence of light branch and bristle as trillions of atoms connect in symmetrical patterns. This miracle of the mineral world, which is also a source of medicine and healing, could not happen in the presence of light.

Most seeds growing in a garden require the absence of light for germination. Protected and enveloped by the soil, the seed rests and soaks up water, slowly beginning to rehydrate. Eventually it swells with such a force that the seed is ruptured, and the seed radicle finally emerges to form the primary root. Only then does the plant body begin to sprout upward toward the sunlight.

Even the living soil itself is dependent on darkness. In the generative darkness of the topsoil, a vibrant interplay between soil microorganisms, minerals, air, and water feed the decomposition from which new life can be cultivated and sustained. Likewise, the process of composting, which is a slow dance between carbon, nitrogen, air, and moisture, produces the nutrient of humus, which ensures the vitamins and minerals our food needs to grow. The cultivation of food is dependent upon unseen microorganisms and beneficial insects that live and thrive in the hearth of the dark topsoil. The alchemy of soil building requires absolute protection from the light.

Darkness carries the invaluable power of that which is slow, resting, often invisible, and still. There is little that light can do to speed up the necessary dormancy of a flower bed in wintertime or the growth cycle of an embryo in the womb. In today's world, however, we undervalue the unseen and slower processes of nature, and we often discount the slower, more passive processes of our own nature. We overvalue light, activity, and speed. Even wintertime, the darkest season of the year that provides periods of silence and quietude, inactivity and sleep for many species, time for introspection for humans, and a general slowing down of life processes is perceived by many as an inconvenience in our lives.

The balance of dark and light, yin and yang, is relevant to all of life. The seed does not remain in darkness forever. It eventually reaches out toward the sunlight and begins the process of photosynthesis. After nine months as a vessel and protector, the muscles of the womb are used with tremendous force to birth a child.

Overlighting the Planet: The Connection between Literal Darkness and Symbolic Darkness

One of the heartbreaks of my lifetime has been witnessing the overlighting of our planet. Just one hundred years ago, physical darkness still prevailed on our planet; but if we look at a satellite image of the planet today, we see that very little darkness is present. We see that most of the planet has been covered in artificial light. Tremendous amounts of fuel have been mined from the earth to light up our environment. Through our assumed need to extract fossil fuel for light and heat, we have caused unprecedented damage to the nocturnal animals and insects of our planet. We have caused light pollution to an extent that has never before been seen. Studies have shown that excessive artificial light has created health issues ranging from an epidemic of insomnia to endocrine disruption. Globally, this overlighting has contributed to an irreversible imbalance to the biosphere that is our home.

Rhythms of day and night are embedded in the biological makeup of all of life. Almost every form of life—plant, animal, human, microbial, insectile—is connected to the Earth spinning on its axis every twenty-four hours. All of life is dependent upon darkness as well as light.

Some of the research on darkness has revealed the following:

- More than 60 percent of the people on the planet and fully 99 percent in the United States and Europe exist under a yellowy lit-up night sky.
- Through these lights our cities can be identified from as far away as the moon.
- Light pollution is most apparent through satellite images of Earth from space. Light emissions have been rising an average rate of 2.2 percent each year since 2012, with emissions growing in some regions as much as 20 percent.
- The 100-watt light bulb, left on every night for a year, is powered by the equivalent of a half-ton of coal.
- Nocturnal animals make up 30 percent of all vertebrates and 60 percent of all invertebrates, and their health has been severely threatened.
- In 2019, researchers reported that West Nile-virus-infected house sparrows inhabiting light-polluted areas were infectious for two

days longer than those birds living in darkness. This increased the risk of a West Nile outbreak by 21 percent.[2]

The excessive lighting of our planet has had detrimental effects on the circadian rhythms that regulate human health, and the use of fossil fuels for artificial lighting has contributed to climate change. It is clear that the global plant, animal, and microbial world has been deeply impacted by the overlighting of the planet, as have the human psyche and spirit.

Waking Up from Marketplace Mentality

Marketplace mentality is the habit of perceiving life not only as subject/object but as consumer/product. It's the perception that all of life is a resource for humans to consume. The consumer looks out at life and assesses, judges, measures, and compares *everything* in order to get the most out of it. For instance, through marketplace mentality, we have justified our overuse of fossil fuels. We perceive fossil fuels solely as a resource to consume, rather than the stored deep dark transformed light of the sun and all organic life. Oil is a sacred remembrance, the condensed energy of all animals and photosynthesizing plant forms that lived and died on planet Earth.

We've come to apply marketplace mentality not only when, for instance, we are shopping and might need to evaluate the value of an item but also in our approach to dating, when we assess someone through a checklist of standards and in communicating transactionally rather than with the intention to connect. At work, marketplace mentality can motivate us to treat our bodies as tools or machines for production. Even spiritual practice is sometimes approached through marketplace mentality, shopping for the most exotic path to enlightenment and then trying to attain the goal of awakening.

The Judeo-Christian implication that light represents good and dark represents evil is thoroughly and subtly infused in today's world. Even the dictionary definition of darkness affirms this bias, defining *darkness* as the "absence or deficiency of light" and "wickedness or evil."[3] The definition continues with references to secrecy, unhappiness, distress or gloom, lack of spiritual or intellectual enlightenment, and ignorance. The Christian Bible references "the deep valley of shadow and death." And in Buddhism, "elemental darkness" refers to the fundamental place of ignorance and unconsciousness in opposition to the awakened state. This facilitates a distorted message to flee that which is dark in favor of that which is light.

The duality of light versus dark and the rejection of darkness is the cornerstone of human suffering. Darkness is neutral. There is no darkness beyond that which is sacred. In order to evolve as a species, we must compassionately examine our relationship to the still, dark, and restorative aspects of nature. We must also forgive, rather than judge, ourselves for having participated for so long in the demonization of darkness and the extreme imbalance it has created within humanity.

The Invitation of Darkness in Wisdom Traditions throughout the World

Physical darkness has been considered a facilitator of growth in spiritual traditions across the globe, throughout centuries of human existence. Many spiritual traditions—from the earliest pagan religions to Christianity—consider physical darkness the original consciousness or "first spirit." I find it fascinating that humans lived on planet Earth for six hundred thousand years before discovering how to make fire, spending half of their existence in the physical darkness.[4] In 1925, only half of the homes in the United States had dependable access to electricity.[5]

Recognizing the power of the living darkness in spiritual practice, ancient and contemporary traditions have utilized the darkness of the night, of caves and caverns, and darkness retreats in rituals that take humans beyond the surface mind and ordinary reality. These rituals are about deepening one's connection to the divine and cultivating spiritual leadership. By practicing in the dark, people are unable to rely on their habitual perception, which generally depends on light to see.

In the words of Simon Buxton and Ross Heaven, "Darkness work is truly cross-cultural. It can be found within Taoist teachings dating back 2,500 years and can be traced to Buddhist, Christian, Hindu, aboriginal, and indigenous traditions. Within many paths and faiths, it is considered a secret—a staggering one that is kept hidden by its very prevalence, for darkness is simultaneously everywhere and nowhere."[6]

Darkness retreats are undertaken in the Tibetan Dzogchen tradition "lasting from hours to years" to enable the practitioner to navigate their transition at the time of death. Through "vision practice," in the sensory deprivation of darkness, the practitioner can experience states of consciousness similar to the bardo states that occur just after death. Similar to the dreams we experience during sleeping states, the practitioner can also receive powerful visions as the contents of the unconscious psyche rise to consciousness.[7]

In ancient Taoist practice,[8] spiritual training could begin with up to two months spent in pure darkness, enabling the student to access freedom from the narrative of the conditioned mind. Similar to the effect of a silent meditation retreat, in which the silence itself creates a mirror for witnessing the conditioned mind more clearly, darkness supports the practitioner in seeing more clearly (and letting go of) the conditioned mind's delusion. The noise and busyness of the conditioned mind appear even louder and more exaggerated against the backdrop of darkness. In the words of the contemporary Taoist master Mantak Chia, "In the Darkness, our mind and soul begin to wander freely in the vast realms of psychic and spiritual experience. When you enter the primordial state or force, you are reunited with the true self and divinity within."[9]

In his book *Of Water and Spirit*, the West African writer and spiritual leader Malidoma Some speaks about the Dagara tribe of Burkina Faso, the tribe he was born into, who also consider darkness to be a powerful living spirit.

Among the Dagara, darkness is sacred. Our night is the day of the Spirit and of the ancestors, who come to us to tell us what lies on our life paths. To have light around you is like saying that you would rather ignore this wonderful opportunity to be shown the way. To the Dagara, such an attitude is inconceivable. The one exception to this rule is a bonfire. Though they omit a powerful glow, they are not prohibited because there is always drumming around them, and the beat of the drum cancels out the light.[10]

In North America, the Lakota Sioux[11] also perceive the living landscape of darkness as the abode of helping spirits. Their most powerful healing ceremony is the *Yuwipi*, which translates as "they wrap him up." In a darkened room or tent, the shaman is tightly wrapped and bound with rope. The shaman is then laid down upon a bed of sagebrush. In the ritual that follows, the shaman is freed from his bonds by his benevolent spirit allies, which often appear in the darkened room as moving or flashing blue lights.[12]

In Japan, within the indigenous spiritual tradition of Shinto,[13] the discipline of seclusion, or *komori*, is practiced in the darkness of a cave, shrine, or temple. For Shinto, spiritual power is seen as manifesting in darkness within a sealed vessel, where it gestates and grows over time. It eventually bursts through its covering, finally emerging into the light of the world, similar to a seed gestating in the dark soil before it emerges into the sunlight.[14]

It is also important to acknowledge Wicca and other neo-pagan and shamanic practices that celebrate darkness as the domain of the deep feminine. In Wicca, for instance, the Triple Goddess represents the cycles of the moon as well as the cycles of a woman's life—maiden, mother, and crone. The Triple Goddess is associated with the wilderness, sexuality, and the cycle of life and death. Darkness is considered a powerful domain of communication with the spirits that support all creation and all healing. It is important to also note that it was this very affiliation with darkness and the deep feminine that led to mass persecution of Wiccan and pagan practitioners.

The Trance of Separation and Hierarchical Perception

Our relationship to dark and light today reflects a deeper and fundamental wound to the human psyche. Through the myth of separation, the conditioned mind stands outside of life labeling, assessing, and measuring everything that we encounter. This filter rejects one half of life.

It is as if we have forgotten who we are free of hierarchical perception—a kind of collective amnesia. The myth of separation has become so well-worn that it can feel like skin. It informs the dominant paradigm and our way of living on planet Earth and has become a loud and consistent distraction from our actual experience of life.

The phrase *dominant paradigm* refers to the cultural mores, worldview, and values that are deeply embedded in the structures of a society. In this historical time, the dominant worldview reflects a combination of perspectives that assume a separatist, mechanistic, individualistic, winner-take-all, consumer-oriented worldview. This worldview has been reinforced by centuries of warfare, racism, and sexism, domination over nature, and corruption of religious "rights." It has been exponentially strengthened by the seventeenth-century Cartesian era, colonialism, imperialism, and the Industrial Revolution. Each of these movements rejected a more holistic, earth-based paradigm that many indigenous cultures and pre-Christian spiritual traditions had known well, based in wholeness rather than separation.

Hierarchy was invented by humankind and creates an unsustainable order of the human mind. In addition to limiting our perceptions, it mandates an artificial code of behavior, societal order, and values—discounting some and prioritizing others. Hierarchical systems of thought discount the innate rightness of being, the intrinsic value of life as it is.

People tend to see hierarchy as an ordering device that provides structure to humankind—yet everyone on the hierarchical ladder suffers, although to varying degrees. Deluded by hierarchical perception, no one is naturally comfortable. No one is free to be what and who they really are at any point on the ladder. Even those at the top rung may live in an underlying state of anxiety and fear; they realize intuitively or subconsciously that their value has been equated with a measurement that could be taken away at any moment.

Yet the collective consciousness polices itself and corrects one another, like a herd of sheep. Regardless of the social order, if someone starts to wander from their place in the hierarchy, they are corrected or rejected. Within the paradigm of hierarchical perception, if you choose to be fully authentic, the essential expression of who you are, you can be made an outcast. You can risk the flock leaving you behind. Or you can be protected by a shared community created by everyone facing the same direction. That is the only way for a human to be recognized and honored within the dominant paradigm.

The most basic Pali translation of *mindfulness* is "to remember." Mindfulness practice is a means of waking up from our collective amnesia. When we return our attention to present-moment compassionate awareness, we remember who we are beyond skewed perception. We remember our original consciousness or innate connection to source. We awaken to the backdrop of interconnection that exists in every moment of our life. This interconnection never leaves us, although we may regularly leave it.

When we rest in darkened stillness, we can see life just as it is—without constantly judging or evaluating our experience as being either good or bad, desirable or undesirable, correct or incorrect. There is no impetus to measure or compare. This awareness is vast, boundless, and all-inclusive—just as the dark night sky wraps her blanket equally over all of life.

Rainer Maria Rilke captures this eloquently in his poem "The Night":

You, darkness, of whom I am born—I love you more than the flame
That limits the world
To the circle it illuminates

And excludes all the rest.
But the dark embraces everything;
Shapes and shadows, creatures and me,
People, nations—just as they are.
It lets me imagine a great presence stirring beside me.
I believe in the night.[15]

Touching the Earth and Choosing Truth

Zoroaster, founder of the world's oldest monotheistic faith, Zoroastrianism, created the polarized universe, good and evil, and the desire for human beings to align with one or the other. This ancient framework is deeply coded into most human languages across the globe today. It is visible in the ways that families, friends, communities, and governments relate to the human experience. It is evident in the lens of judgment and criticism through which most humans evaluate themselves and in their fear of inadequacy and fear of rejection. In this age when human polarization has reached an extreme, it is imperative to inquire into the nature of this collective narrative.

What motivates our presumption that good and evil are the bottom line? Because we have internalized the separation of the two—light as good and dark as evil—we project this divide outward. Our constant projection and polarization regarding good and evil, light and dark keep us from taking responsibility for the nature of our minds, and rather than owning and healing the cause of our inner divide, we allow it to become the lens through which we evaluate the world and others.

The human ego thrives amid drama and polarization. In order to validate our experiences as a separate self, quantifying one's experience through rationalization, our stories and internal narrative require an element of drama. Evil demons, difficult challenges, and dark forces to be battled are often an underlying part of the inner narrative.

In the story of Buddha sitting under the Bodhi tree, while the Buddha is taunted by the demon Mara with every distraction, delusion, and seduction he could come up with, the Buddha remained still, acknowledging that this demon existed only in his own mind. He further acknowledged that everything humans fear is projected into the imaginal world onto demonic forces and that we each have a conscious choice in every moment to awaken from this.

In deep frustration at the Buddha's lack of response, Mara finally exclaimed, "By whose authority are you able to say no to every attempt I make to distract you and pull you into suffering? By whose authority do you stand in your own power?"

The Buddha reached down and touched the earth and said, "By the authority of the earth."

The imperative of collective awakening is to touch the earth and acknowledge the demons that we project into the imaginal world through the misperception of darkness. The moment that we feed hierarchical perception, we abandon truth. We miss out on seeing ourselves and one another clearly. We miss knowing the beauty of the complex caves and subterranean caverns of human consciousness.

Some people have caused tremendous harm. Some people have extreme obstacles covering up their heart, but the nature of the heart is to be always open. Hurt people hurt. Healed people heal. Yet everyone you will ever meet has a fundamental need to connect, to belong, to be seen, and to feel loved. We are in this together.

* * *

MINDFUL INQUIRY

How often do you spend time in pure physical darkness? What do you love and savor about the dark? How do you find rest and refuge, mystery, thrill, or creative inspiration in physical darkness? What becomes available or possible for you only in the dark?

Think of a memorable experience or time in your life in which you communed with the divine darkness. Perhaps camping outside beneath the open sky? Stargazing? Walking along the beach at night? Then consider the ways that your ancestral lineage—dharmic or karmic—celebrated darkness.

What is your relationship to artificial light? Is there a balance in your life between physical light and dark? Is there a balance between activity and restoration? Please notice what feelings arise as you reflect on these questions.

*   *   *

EXPERIENTIAL PRACTICE: BRINGING AWARENESS
TO HIERARCHICAL PERCEPTION

Please find a fresh page in your journal so that you can take notes throughout this exercise. This is an invitation to pay attention, throughout an entire twenty-four-hour cycle of your life, to the myriad ways your mind perceives through hierarchical perception. There is no need to bring judgment to this investigation. Instead, bring compassionate awareness to your thoughts and mind habits, noticing the number of times that your mind labels life through hierarchical perception. For instance, good/bad, superior/inferior, higher/lower, better/worse, light/dark, positive/negative, special/not special. How often do these labels arise? You might notice obvious hierarchies, and you might notice subtler ones. Observing one's own mind can be a humbling practice. I encourage you to meet this investigation with both sincerity and a light heart. Each time you find your mind labeling through hierarchical perception, ask yourself, Is this really so? What does this assumption actually serve? What is my experience, in this moment, if I let go of this assumption? *Take in a deep breath. Let that thought go and see if you can meet what is with compassionate neutrality rather than hierarchical perception.*

PART TWO

Fruitful Darkness and the Realm of Emotional Intelligence

The chapters in this part offer teachings about fierce compassion and emotional intelligence. What are the repercussions of perceiving some human emotions as negative and "dark"? How can such challenging emotions become messengers and a threshold to spiritual growth and a more courageous embrace of our humanity? How do we identify and move beyond spiritual bypassing? This part also explores the cultural habit of "sunshining" and invites a way of living that celebrates turning toward rather than away from those emotions and aspects of ourselves that we label "dark."

3

Fierce Compassion

The Mother of Endarkenment

Obstacles do not interrupt the path, obstacles are the path.

TIBETAN VAJRAYANA BUDDHIST TEACHING[1]

THE FIRST THING THAT OCCURRED when I moved to the monastery was that a quality of primal volcanic anger emerged that I had not been conscious of before. I had nurtured for years a strong identity as a kind, easygoing, and anger-free person. At the monastery, I met Electra. This was the name I gave to a fierce, fuming, outraged, and flammable part of me that suddenly appeared. She was electric with anger, and her feelings were magnified by the silence. This was not an experience I was used to. At that time, I labeled anger as an emotion that was not only dark but also dangerous.

I remember being given a working meditation list one day that included cleaning the outhouses, digging a trench in rocky soil, and learning to do carpentry for the first time. I loved working with my hands and had moved to the monastery knowing that I would be doing working meditation on the land every day, but suddenly, these tasks felt like harsh punishments. The schedule felt oppressive, and I imagined I was being unfairly judged, as evidenced by these challenging assignments. Although I was simply being asked to do working meditation, anchoring in my body and breath in the present moment, it felt to me as if I were being unfairly singled out and persecuted.

At first, I felt deep shame about this anger, which I thought of as a spiritual failure. Because I didn't know what to do with the intensity of energy pulsing through my body, I drew on old habits and attempted to push Electra away. In the quietude of the monastery, I quickly realized how destructive rejecting the anger was. I sensed that the habit of pushing away a whole part of my psyche to be complicit with a culture of appearances—which meant for me presenting a calm and accepting demeanor to the world—had inadvertently allowed resentment to build up within me. I sensed that it was useless to try to hide my anger, as it was evident through my body language to any perceptive person.

Finally, in a personal guidance session with my Zen teacher, I talked about Electra. I shared that I felt sorry and ashamed to be bringing such "dark feelings" to the monastery. My teacher remained calm and warm, not offended in the least, as I'd feared she would be. She spoke to me instead with a clear understanding that quickly dissipated the shame I had been carrying.

"Have you ever really spent time with this part of you? Have you listened to all that Electra has to say? Have you let yourself fully feel the energy Electra carries, staying present as these feelings pulse through your body? What a perfect moment in your life to get to know and befriend Electra. Electra is in desperate need of a companion she can trust. She has been diminished and ignored for far too long. Meditate with her fire. Dig in the earth and sweat with her. Listen to her and feel her burning embers in your body. She is a sacred messenger and receiving her message requires friendship."

And so, I set out to become acquainted with Electra, free of judgment, with the possibility that perhaps I could meet this anger I perceived as a personal failure with welcome. Meditating with Electra without resisting the negative and destructive thoughts and feelings she evoked, I began to feel a deep settling. *There was vast relief in realizing that it was OK to not feel OK.* I harnessed Electra's energy through the sweat and toil of building raised garden beds. I let her speak to me unedited and unconstrained through written words, and I genuinely listened. I danced with her, giving Electra full permission to take bold and unbridled shape through my body without needing to make sense of her expression. As I spent time with this untamed energy, feeling intense emotions move through my entire being, I began to realize that this anger came from an ancient source. It was a natural response to witnessing the world's suffering and corruption and an energy that I could perhaps learn to utilize skillfully.

Part of healing was the realization that my anger had a valid reason for its existence. It felt far greater than my lifetime, and I understood it as the collective outrage of all beings who had witnessed the profound harm caused by greed, hatred, and delusion. Over time, this anger had been woven into my living DNA.

This anger was directly related to my ancestors, who, as Jews, had been severely persecuted and their numbers decimated, and to all of life on earth. In the culture in which I grew up, there seemed to me to be an ominous shadow cast upon anger or negative emotions. In an effort to repress my own feelings of anger, I had not learned how to fuel my anger into empowerment.

Finally, the one needing healing was no longer hidden beneath a hardened shield and could be met with the welcome she longed for. Like a sea creature lying safe within its shell, a soft, more vulnerable, often powerless aspect of the psyche exists beneath the protective covering of anger. I could thank my anger for trying to protect me while trusting it was no longer needed, and I learned to perceive Electra as a beautiful teacher. The reward was an empowering new level of emotional integration, self-acceptance, resilience, and wholeness. I remembered, as if waking up from a trance, that I am not my anger. *I am the fierce compassion that can be with it.*

What a gift to make the shift from being burdened by and ashamed of my anger to letting it reveal the path to healing. I finally understood that emotional darkness is not a problem to be hidden or repaired. Emotions can be messengers, inviting us to travel deep down into the underground landscape of our psyche, collective history, and human trauma in order to unlock healing.

By reclaiming my ability to feel fully, I also reclaimed a vastly broader spectrum of my emotional experience. I had judged and disowned so many emotions rather than given them their rightful place within me. In turning toward the perceived darkness, I began to feel empowered with a dramatically new degree of vitality, peace, courage, belonging, and truth telling.

When I finally went down and into my body to embrace the dark power of anger, I began to realize its message: Take a stand and speak up on life's behalf, no matter what. Be a dignified truth teller regardless of the consequences. Be willing to be outraged when it serves life. It matters not what other people think. Recognize that this burning fire that is within you is fierce compassion. It is a fire of creation as well as destruction. Allow it to burn through the obstacles on your path and use you as a vessel for love on behalf of all beings.

The Imperative of Fierce Compassion

Compassion does not exist outside of us. It's not a concept we can access through rational thought or philosophizing. It's an innate force within each and every one of us. It is unwavering love and protection for life, or the courage of our shared heart. When we turn toward rather than away from that which we perceive as dark, difficult, or absent of light, then our compassion is unlocked. Compassion is found in being willing to venture beyond our comfort zones and walk through the portals of discomfort, pain, and vulnerability for ourselves or another.

Compassion expresses to another person (or to aspects of one's self), *You are not alone; your pain is tethered to my experience. I am right here with you no matter what. I am not judging you. I am not turning away.* Sometimes we are required to offer this expression of generosity to ourselves and sometimes to others, but it is the steadfast and unwavering nature of this expression that allows for healing to organically occur. It is through the perception of being alone or isolated that we suffer as human beings. Compassion seeks out and welcomes that which has been ignored, left out, or pushed away into isolation.

Sometimes compassion is gentle, as in the soft receptivity we experience when someone listens to us fully without imposing their opinion or agenda. Sometimes it is bold, such as the willingness to speak up courageously and honestly on behalf of consciousness. Skillful protesting that expresses nonviolence is an example of fierce compassion. This has been modeled by a wide range of spiritual and political leaders and activists, including Martin Luther King Jr.; Mahatma Gandhi; Greta Thunberg, the Swedish environmental activist; Opal Tometi, cofounder of Black Lives Matter; and many others. When we firmly anchor ourselves in the intention to respond compassionately to life, there is a full spectrum of expression that compassion can take.

Fierce compassion may take the form of consciously setting a needed boundary in an unhealthy relationship dynamic or firmly saying no to our own deluded and harmful thoughts. Even showing up for a daily meditation practice requires the fierce compassion of discipline and fortitude. It takes unrelenting love to honor the choice we have in every moment to remember who we really are in a world that rewards unconsciousness. Closing one's eyes and going along with the status quo can be a means of fitting into a dysfunctional society. People who act from fierce compassion have been judged, punished, and burned at the stake throughout human history.

Fierce compassion is the mother of endarkenment; it is the courage that expresses our willingness to stay present in the dark and to let the darkness open our heart's perception. In the words of Carl Jung, "One does not become enlightened by imagining figures of light, but by making the darkness conscious."[2] I take this to mean that every time we welcome—rather than push away—what we have judged, rejected, feared, or neglected, we activate fierce compassion. When we consciously go down and into our bodies, our emotions, and our unmetabolized pain, we can remember our innate capacity for love.

It takes fierce compassion to take the next step forward even when there seems to be nothing lighting a dark unknown landscape. Endarkenment is about unlocking our heart's perception in order to remember how to meet life with unrelenting love in every situation we encounter.

Fierce compassion cannot go along with injustice or choose complicity with collective conditioning so as not to rock the boat. Fierce compassion calls forth authenticity and sometimes audacity. It is nonviolent. It never causes harm, but it might call upon outrageousness. It knows how to take a stand and how to say no with dignity.

Sometimes we become confused in spiritual practice, because we've been fed so many ideas about being nice and how that should look. We might diminish our true voice in order to sound pleasant. We might abandon our own needs not out of genuine service but to seek approval. Or we might repress or discount a difficult emotion in order to appear more acceptable to others. We might hear ourselves saying yes to another commitment even when our whole body is telling us no. We might try to cheer someone up without really honoring their actual pain and underlying need for empathy.

Fierce compassion is always kind, but it is not necessarily nice. It does not perceive you and me as separate, so there is no justification for caretaking or tiptoeing around one another. Spiritual practice is not about trying to attain a standard of enlightenment; it's about reawakening to meet life with a strong spine and open heart simultaneously.

Fierce compassion is all-inclusive: it does not exclude either the light or the dark. We hinder our capacity for emotional intelligence each time we turn away from or numb out difficult feelings because we deem them dark and therefore negative. The label *dark* becomes an excuse to push something away or deny its existence.

Why is it our collective responsibility in today's world to embrace our emotions? Consider that when you were born, you inherited in your DNA, in your ovaries or gonads, in the cellular memory of your body, in your genetic configuration, all the pain, trauma, and grief of your family lineage. Consider that you, as a human being, are carrying the history of your human ancestry. As a collective, these are times of tremendous distortion, violence, and xenophobia. The human species has an unprecedented amount of shared grief that has remained stored within—but not integrated into—our being. It is the grief of generations of racism, patriarchy, and misogyny. It is the grief of a profound disconnect from nature. It is the grief of global suffering and inequity. We all carry within us the grief of the myth of separation and its detrimental impact on the planet and all living things.

We have also inherited a tremendous capacity for joy, love, healing, and vibrant aliveness. But grief and joy are two sides of the same coin. If we repress one, we suppress the other.

This Too Is Welcome

In the culture I grew up in, anger was not an acceptable emotion to exhibit. Even in the early Buddhist teachings I experienced, the message I received was, *Do not be angry*. It was only later that I learned of the subtler nuances of this instruction. In actuality, Buddhism offers a path for being with difficult emotions without taking them personally or identifying with them; the teaching to not be angry is often given as the justification to ignore or repress anger. Through the duality of light and dark, for example, meditators sometimes bypass primal and animalistic emotions, including outrage, ecstasy, and desire, to attempt to elevate themselves to spiritual light or purity.

At the monastery I began to experience a profound sense of relief when I realized there was nothing to turn away from. Nothing was inherently "dark" and thus nothing required my judgment or rejection. The more I meditated, the more I accessed a strong and steadfast presence within myself. It confirmed, *This too is welcome. Your pain, your disappointment, your resistance, your grouchiness, your broken heart. Whatever arises belongs here and can be met with love.* I had been starving for space to *be with* and welcome my human experience, free from the habit of labeling and judgment and free from other people's interference.

To be free from the insistent heliotropic tendency to move toward the sun is the invitation of endarkenment. I finally gave myself permission to cease the restless activity of chasing light. I could perceive the shadows within my human experience as equally sacred.

Love in the context of spiritual practice means to welcome life with respect, openness, gentle curiosity, and kindness. It does not refer to an elevated state of bliss or the commercialized idea of a heart-shaped box of chocolates. Instead of trying to push away the dark, love becomes the entire focus of spiritual inquiry. We learn how to meet aspects of the psyche—anger, fear, jealousy, anxiety, or laziness—with compassion. We learn to befriend those parts of us—and of others—that we previously deemed unexceptional, weak, wounded, reactive, defensive, and far from perfect. We begin to experience inner alchemy and the transformation of aspects of our lives that before had seemed to us to be negative and unworthy.

Remembering the Sacred Partnership of Light and Dark

Anger becomes power when we are willing to hold it in stillness and transmute it through our physical bodies as an expression of love. Being human involves experiencing disappointment, discomfort, loss, grief, heartbreak, illness, and death. Life, for each of us, carries pain beyond what we can conceive of or think we can bear. It also involves love and beauty beyond our imagination. Life is full of possibility. This is the paradox of being human. When we label natural human experiences as dark, we justify abandoning ourselves or one another in the most difficult times. We justify closing our hearts in those moments of greatest need.

We pretend that we can make our pain go away. But instead, we lock our pain in a dungeon deep within where it hardens and sickens us. We hide our unmetabolized grief in the only place in which it cannot be met with love. Fierce compassion is the force that can excavate these caverns in our collective psyche. We have inherited generations upon generations of collective trauma that humanity has perpetuated for thousands of years. When we put that which we dislike into the chasm we label *darkness*, darkness becomes the hidden locked container for all of our shadows. Through seeking out the forbidden and unwanted spaces within our collective psyche, we can meet our collective heartbreak with love and healing.

Lama Rod Owens, a Tibetan Buddhist teacher who guides collective grief work, suggests that we cannot wake up until we are willing to let go of the idea of utopia. The word *utopia* derives from the Greek *ou-topos*, meaning "nowhere" or "no place." Meditation practice invites us to bring awareness to our fixation with this idealized nowhere—the fixation with a perfect, better, more positive life experience that we could and should be experiencing. The habit of pitting an imagined, perfect reality against life as it is, or ourselves as we are, maintains a delusion.[3]

It is by staying present to what is that we find a freedom far greater than the utopia we are seeking. We can stand in unity with ourselves and one another, offering the fierce compassion that says, *I am here with you no matter what.* We can feel our grief together.

As human beings, we continually experience the cycle of expansion and contraction, up and down, beginning and ending, birth and death, light and dark. Yet we fault ourselves for what is the natural process of being alive. Free from the burden of labeling everything as either "positive" or "negative," there is just life happening. Through practice we remember that we are not our ever-changing emotions or thoughts, but the fiercely compassionate embrace that welcomes all of it.

The Verdant Cavern of the Underworld

In order to rise

From its own ashes

A phoenix

First

Must

Burn.

OCTAVIA BUTLER[4]

So much of Western cosmology, Hollywood, and modern theistic religion perpetuates an image of the underworld as dark, ominous, and forbidden. Humans constantly associate the underworld with hell, the domain of monsters, demons, and evil in all of its manifestations. Ironically, hell in its formal depiction is actually a brightly lit environment, constantly consumed by fire. In actuality, there is not anything substantially physically dark about our depiction of hell.

I believe that our fear of the human underworld—the dark place deep within us—is actually fear of authentic power. Authentic power is something I will be exploring in future chapters of this book. My experience, again and again, is that when we go deep down into our bodies and the innermost caverns of our psychological-emotional underworld, alchemical healing is made possible. When we are taught to avoid our personal underworlds, we are taught to avoid transformation. By being willing to stay present outside our comfort zones, however, we activate our *discomfort resiliency*. This is the resiliency and vitality gained only by turning *toward* rather than *away* from our discomfort.

Our inner light is often revealed to us deep in the trenches of our emotional and psychological depths. When we are willing to excavate the underworld, without fearing its darkness, we can find myriad gems that exist in the dark concealed caverns and shadows of our beings.

The anger I had to come face to face with at the monastery became an ally of truth, accountability, love, and perseverance in my life. It has been with me since as a source of energy and vitality from which to access courage when I am unsure or afraid. It has nourished my willingness to love well and model shared power. I experience it, often, as feeling encircled by my ancestors cheering me on through the challenges of being human, reminding me to love on behalf of us all.

Meeting the Messy Parts with Fierce Compassion

On meditation retreats, there is always someone who asks, "A painful feeling is disrupting my retreat. I came here for peace but instead, there is a sadness, an anxiety, or an anger that feels unbearable to me. What can I do?" I remind that person that there is nothing wrong with those feelings. I suggest that this is a golden opportunity to soften judgment and spend some time willingly getting to know this part of themselves.

We hold many assumptions about difficult emotions and too often consider them shameful or weak. We may even believe that they will overwhelm us. The alternative is to activate deep listening and curiosity. Welcoming difficult emotions is easier than we think. We can allow ourselves to feel. We can allow ourselves to be. Just as we develop trust in a new friendship when we are met repetitively by the other person with openness, kindness, and safety, we develop friendship with ourselves. The first step is always to replace judgment with curiosity and listen to this aspect of our being without judgment. This is how we claim the freedom of the heart. We can only find it by accepting and embracing life (and ourselves) as it already is.

One means for beginning to excavate or explore difficult emotions is through *mindful inquiry. Mindful inquiry* is the practice of inquiring into our actual experience in the moment and holding our questions with openness and receptivity rather than trying to fix, solve, or change our experience. In this introspective process, there is no need to grasp for an answer. In inquiry, we simply hold our question gently, sensing and feeling into it. By turning *toward* our direct experience, we allow for our awareness to gradually open in an emergent way. I sometimes describe this as becoming a Zen detective—relaxed and in the moment but paying subtle investigative attention. With difficult emotions, the inquiry begins with an exploration of what is happening in our body, mind, and feelings in a subtle way, in the moment.

∗　∗　∗

MINDFUL INQUIRY

When you experience difficult emotions, what is arising in your mind? What is the lens through which you are perceiving? What are you believing about yourself, another, or the world in that moment?

What is happening in your physical body? Where do you feel this emotion in your body and what sensations are present? Can you simply notice these sensations and accept them?

What is happening in your emotional body? Can you welcome these feelings without pushing them away?

Sometimes, gently inquiring into our difficult emotions allows for a softening and a shift in how we perceive them. We remember, by turning to our direct experience, that we are not our emotions but the awareness that holds them. Sometimes, we sense the need to inquire more deeply. We might ask, Who is this part of me? *And in response, we might notice quite clearly,* This is a scared five-year-old *or* This is the driven one, taking over my whole body with a sense of urgency. *We can also ask,* What is the need not being met for this part of me? Is there a reassurance or expression of genuine compassion that this suffering part of me needs?

Without trying to solve, fix, or change the experience of this aspect of our psyche, we can tune in to our genuine compassion, just as we would for a friend or child we love who is suffering. Sometimes there are specific words of loving-

kindness and reassurance that arise. Sometimes there is a clear instruction or remedy that arises when we witness and listen to ourselves in this way.

This quality of kind and nonjudgmental investigation opens up our perception, and we see more clearly. Returning to the example of Electra, through witnessing the hurt and feelings of powerlessness beneath her anger, I was able to feel for her suffering and sense exactly what she needed. I was able to understand how often she had diminished her own truth for others and show her another possibility. I was able to meet her with the care and precision that she needed rather than just apply a one-size-fits-all blanket of kindness over her. She felt completely seen and heard. Practice can both heal our trauma and enable us to remember that we are already whole. Alongside our trauma, there exists true nature already intact, holding us where we are smooth and where we are cracked.

In a text from the Kashmir Shaivist tradition, it is stated, "There is no darkness within. Only light unseen. Deep within you is the great eastern Sun that never sets."[5] We realize this unseen light each time we are willing to turn toward rather than away from that which we perceive as the absence of light.

The Dharma Gate of Historical Trauma and Global Uncertainty

The *bodhisattva vow* in Soto Zen Buddhism includes the phrase, "Dharma gates are boundless; I vow to enter them." In every moment, we have an opportunity to align our actions with consciousness and to act on behalf of all beings—past, present, and future.

The complex, overactive, individually focused, and unsustainable world in which I lived prior to the monastery was mirrored within the habits of my own mind. My outer activism merged with my inner work as I began to take responsibility for the habits and patterns of my own mind. I began to understand that meditation was not only the gateway to personal liberation but also to collective evolution.

There is a popular tendency in today's world toward *spiritual materialism,* or the use of meditation or other spiritual paths to attain a temporary state of bliss. An expansive moment can be mistaken as a refuge from suffering. Through spiritual materialism, we might use meditation to find a moment of peace or expanded consciousness, but without opening our hearts to the suffering of our world, for that would make us uncomfortable. Through *spiritual materialism*, it is easy to see taking responsibility as a burden rather than an expression of liberation. Because taking responsibility might make us feel uncomfortable or helpless (or, let's face it, be inconvenient), we turn away. In so doing, we can easily delude ourselves and fail to see the opportunity that is right in front of us.

Endarkenment invites us to open our hearts to the dharma gate that exists just behind inconvenience and comfort. Every invitation we are given to take responsibility—for ourselves, others, or the planet—is a dharma gate. We have known since the 1970s, for instance, that climate change needed to be addressed, yet we did not do so. We have known for decades that our cities were in need of redesign and new infrastructure in the face of our expanding population and changing climate, yet we avoided the task at hand. Here in the United States, we have allowed four hundred years of systemic racism to continue to inform our policies and entire way of life.

It is popular to dabble in spiritual teachings without ever surrendering to unconditional love. The real opportunity is to *be* the *fierce compassion* that expresses our love for all of life. *Fierce compassion* transforms grief into the primeval compost that feeds restorative and regenerative action on behalf of life. The healing we are asked to address as a collective requires our discomfort resiliency. It requires that we learn to turn *toward* rather than *away* from our suffering and take responsibility for long-term and *inconvenient* vision rather than short-term fixes. It requires that we ask fresh questions, grounded in presence, and remain open for guidance. It requires us to let go of the eternal summer and celebrate wintertime too.

The next steps to endarkenment include the following:

Turn toward rather than away from that which you label dark.

Replace judgment with living curiosity. Replace labeling with inquiry.

Consider that by labeling something as "dark" and unwanted, you place it in a dungeon of isolation. Bring it instead, not into the light that judges, but into the soft embrace of darkened stillness. True darkness perceives everything as belonging and meets everything with love. It is the fierce compassion that turns nothing and no one away.

∗   ∗   ∗

MINDFUL INQUIRY

How have you experienced turning away from perceived darkness within yourself, only to find that what you were turning away from was a sacred messenger? What teachings or wisdom have been revealed to you when you were willing to stay present with perceived darkness within and meet it with curiosity rather than judgment?

How have you and how do you express fierce compassion in your life? How is the current state of our world both challenging you to the core and encouraging/inspiring you to open your heart with fierce compassion? What current situation in your life is calling for fierce compassion? How does it feel in your body to acknowledge this?

How have you experienced the difference between "being nice" and "being kind"? What experiences have you had when another person treated you unkindly or inauthentically but through the guise of being nice? Was there a time you have justified being unkind to yourself in order to be nice to someone else? How does it feel to acknowledge this?

∗   ∗   ∗

EXPERIENTIAL PRACTICE: REVERENCE FOR THE DARK MYSTERY

You can either sit or lie down for this practice, as long as you are comfortable. Close your eyes or use a blindfold. Rest in darkened stillness for a couple of minutes, relaxing and breathing deeply. Then imagine that there is a window

in front of you. This window is open not to the outside world but to pure dark-
ness. Like the night sky, you can sense the entire universe, the divine mystery,
through this window. Notice how it feels to gaze directly into the dark. You
might feel curiosity or tenderness, serenity, or exhilaration. Remember that you
are safe here. And you can open your eyes at any time.

Now, place your hand on your heart to evoke compassion. Feel warmth and
kindness emanating through this gesture toward yourself and then feel your
compassion toward and reverence for the darkness, the unknown. Without
needing to know/see visually who might receive it, send the compassion from
your heart directly into the darkness itself. You might allow words, poetry, or
blessings to arise as an offering to the darkness.

Many of us are used to extending compassion toward those forms of life we
can see. How does it feel to offer it to the mystery itself?

You are also welcome to ask for compassion from the darkness. Be still and
allow yourself to receive any expression—through energy, image, words, or met-
aphor—that might arise.

When you feel complete, take in a few deep breaths and gently open your
eyes. What did you notice? How might the invitation to offer compassion to
and reverence for the mystery itself inform more of your everyday life?

4

Entering the
Twilight Temple

Honoring Our Pain for Our World

If we deny our ugliness, we lessen our beauty. If we deny our fear,
we minimize our courage. If we deny our greed, we reduce our generosity.
Our full magnitude is more than most of us can ever imagine.

DEBBIE FORD[1]

I GREW UP IN METROPOLITAN LOS ANGELES, and while I came from an unconventional family of artists, activists, and freethinkers, the California culture we lived in was steeped in the practice of what I call *sunshining*. *Sunshining* points to a cultural focus on the external world and the idea of chasing pleasure and satisfaction in that external world. It is the domain that measures happiness and success based on how things "appear" and the conditioned standards people are supposed to strive to attain. There is a strong message in the dominant paradigm that everything "light" is good and acceptable and everything "dark" is unacceptable. It values positivity, happiness, feeling good, and keeping it light, while rejecting that which might be difficult but also real and human.

Within the culture of sunshining, I regularly witnessed people avoiding certain emotions and honest conversations. I also witnessed people discounting complexity and depth in order to remain on the surface. In order to survive, I learned to mask the parts of me that felt insecure, sensitive, or weak. This required that I monitor, measure, and compare myself to an imagined standard of happiness. I learned to abandon my deeper feelings to keep up appearances and assumed something was wrong with me for being so sensitive to the world's pain. I also learned to be hyperaware of what the external standards and expectations were so that I could meet them and avoid rejection.

In the fall of 1984, when I was eleven years old and had just begun sixth grade, a friend's parents drove my sister and me to the hospital where my dad shared that he had one month to live. His doctor announced, one day out of the blue, that the mole on the left side of my father's back had been misdiagnosed. Although labeled benign almost two years earlier, it was, in fact, malignant melanoma. It was too late to do anything about it, and my family was hit by the avalanche of impermanence. Acknowledging the reality that we would be saying goodbye decades sooner than we had ever imagined, my family broke down in an embrace of tears, love, and immeasurable heartbreak.

Gratefully, we were given three full months together to transition to forever losing life as we had known it. In the period before my father died, between December 1984 to February 1985, his contemplative practice and generosity of spirit shone through within our community. He facilitated meaningful closure with each of his close friends and family members. He hosted gatherings around our fireplace for the children whom he had coached on soccer teams and mentored for many years, helping them to process this experience of loss. He created recordings on cassette tapes that I hold in my treasure chest today. He took long walks with his children, first alongside us and, as he became more fragile, in a wheelchair that my eight-year-old sister liked to push along the cracked sidewalks of our neighborhood. Just weeks before he passed, we drove up the California coast together for our last family trip where we collected seashells, moonstone, and sand dollars along the rocky shores of the San Simeon coastline.

My father died in the middle of the night on February 13, 1985—nestled in the soft covers of his own bed, with my mother, younger sister, and I snuggling at his sides. It was 4:00 a.m., and after hours of listening to his breathing slow down and become sparser as I pretended to sleep, I felt him take his final breath.

Throughout his dying process, I continued to attend school, hang out with my friends, and "go through the motions" of daily life, while feeling grief unlike any I had ever experienced before. I grew up with the same circle of friends from kindergarten through high school and was lucky to have such a close-knit community, but there were remarkably few people around me who actually had a clue about how to support me in my grief. My sixth-grade teacher, who had also lost her own dad as a child, was the one exception. She offered me a journal to record my feelings in, affirming a safe nonjudgmental space and a sense of solidarity with the confusion, shock, and overwhelming sadness that engulfed me. This was the beginning of a lifelong practice of journaling, writing, drawing, and dreaming to help me integrate my emotions and the subconscious.

On the night of my dad's funeral, my younger sister and I slept at a friend's house with our closest girlfriends. My mother needed a rest, and my friends were encouraged to help cheer me up. We were preteens and liked mischief, so on that night we tiptoed downstairs to sneak cookies from the pantry, steal a bra from the teenage sister and put it in the freezer, and toilet paper a neighbor's house. I remember the aftermath of my father's funeral as feeling surreal. Despite the good intentions of my friends, I gave birth to a part of me then who could numb out to pain at will. I learned how to use food, socializing, or reading to stifle feelings that my world was not safe. I had lost the core source of security in my life and had to face fears I had not known before.

I learned then how to go through the motions that everything was okay, to fit in with the community. I began to understand that "good times" were the preferred state of connection. I learned then to put a smile on my face in every circumstance, even while shedding tears inside.

What I actually needed then was permission to grieve for as long as it took to move through loss as a sacred rite of passage. I did not need the modeling of "appearing to be OK" but real support for bringing closure to life as I had known it. I had experienced loss before, when my grandparents and uncle were killed by a drunk driver on a curvy mountain road a few years prior. But this was different. This was my father. I needed guidance on how to inhabit my body and stay present through tumultuous earth-shaking emotions I had never before felt, as I witnessed my father's body sicken and decay. I needed support for integrating the lessons of loss, and I needed guidance as I stepped into the unknown to meet an entirely new and unfamiliar phase of life. Above all, I needed to understand that death was as natural as birth. I needed reassurance that I would be OK without the companionship and protection of my father.

The Call to Awaken

My dad was my first spiritual teacher. He was a contemplative Christian, yoga practitioner, and humanitarian who modeled receptivity. My father never made a lot of money. We lived simply and sometimes struggled to pay for groceries. But he knew what mattered and knew how to laugh. He worked as a social worker and was an attentive listener, always making the people around him feel that they had his full attention. He arose early every morning to do yoga before it became popular and to take a run in the park. He had a twinkle in his eye and a steady compassionate presence in which I could always find support.

When I turned six, inspired by an article about the plight of children and families in Skid Row, twenty minutes away from our home, my mother put her career as an artist on hold to dedicate herself passionately to social justice work in Los Angeles's Skid Row. My dad took over the domain of nurture and relationship in our household. He took care of cooking meals and preparing our school lunches, mentoring and playing with us, and walking us to and from school, and he laid the ground for our spirituality. My parents were hippies in a mixed Jewish-Christian household. We were taught that having a spiritual path was the most important thing, but that it was our choice what form the path would take. My dad exposed me to different religions and philosophies, including the teachings of Krishnamurti, Gautama Buddha, Jesus, St. Francis, Lao Tzu, and myriad other spiritual teachers. He read to me often from his favorite book, *Jonathan Livingston Seagull* by Richard Bach. He made time for real conversations, helping me to recognize the importance of my own insights. Most importantly, he taught me to ask deep questions. Watching my dad bring graceful closure to his life and recognizing the significance of the end-of-life process solidified the values my dad had taught me to live by. Right relationship. Kindness. Service. Integrity. Reverence for Nature and Spirit.

I remember resting with my dad in Griffith Park, the largest city park in Los Angeles. We would hike among oak trees, sage, yucca, and manzanitas, along trails that would open up from desert valleys into vast vistas framing the entire shimmering city of Los Angeles and the blue ocean beyond. We lay on our backs in a field of green grass one afternoon and snacked on trail mix and chocolate. I felt safe in the irreplaceable way a daughter can feel with her father. My dad voiced, "Just looking at the golden sunlight emanating on the blades of grass, how can one not see that Spirit or God is everywhere? How can one not sense the consciousness that is in everything?" He was not necessarily speaking of a theistic God, but the spirit of nature that animates life.

It was this awareness—that all of nature is alive, that all of life is animate—that drew me ultimately to Buddhism and European shamanism. It was this awareness—of God as nature—that opened my perception from a young age to other forms of life and communication. It is not just the visible natural world that lives—the mountains, the trees, the clouds, and the ocean. My experience was that all of life was animate, even those aspects we do not visually see. If nothing else, knowing that all of life is sentient makes it our imperative to engage with life in reverence and care.

My dad opened my eyes continually and constantly to the spiritual dimension beyond what we see visually, and this unnamed field guided my path. Even though the years ahead were tumultuous, I had the basic understanding that we are in this together, humans in partnership with the invisible realm. I also knew that life was fleeting and that there was no time to waste.

On my father's deathbed, very soon before he entered the dark void of the world beyond this world, he held my hand and shared with firm conviction, "Yours will be a path of enlightenment. Of this I am certain." While I did not fully understand the meaning of enlightenment back then, these words from my father helped me to trust the mysterious unfolding of my path going forth. My dad did not say this to make me feel special or spiritually entitled. He said it to affirm my true nature, which is the job of any good spiritual teacher. His words inspired me to listen, humbly, to a calling within that I always felt leading me. He encouraged me to ask deep questions and think outside the box.

Society's message that happiness came from making money, gaining fame, chasing pleasure, or winning never made sense to me. These messages were constant and loud in the world surrounding me, but my dad's final message supported me to continually question conventionally accepted reality. It led me over time to expand my path of enlightenment to include the relational realm of endarkenment.

The Road to Recovery

My family did not recover easily from my father's death. The years that ensued, my teenage years, carried a great deal of additional difficulty and adversity. While I was lucky to have a community to be part of, and we had a roof over our heads and food on the table, I often felt alone. I had always been more sensitive and intuitive than the other kids in my peer group, but now I was aware of how fleeting life is in a world that did not seem to acknowledge it. While my family never named it directly, I think we felt constant pressure to make sure we appeared OK. It seemed as if we somehow had to prove that we had transcended our loss.

In my mother's words, her kids raised themselves from that point on, while she coped by working around the clock as a dedicated social justice activist. I learned to keep myself busy. I experienced an impenetrable grief as a tight lump in my throat for many years and developed a secret eating disorder to cope.

My mom was a visionary activist whose dedicated response to the pain of our world also informed my life. She was unapologetically loud and pushy, and I received the gift of witnessing her tenacious efforts impact the lives of hundreds and then thousands of people. Her work grew nationally and internationally, but it also cast a shadow over our family. I internalized her assumption that the underlying grief of loss was too overwhelming to face directly.

Simultaneously, throughout my childhood I spent a significant amount of time on Skid Row, where my mom's nonprofit for helping homeless families was initially located. It was there that I witnessed basic human needs—access to healthy food, shelter, and sanitization—not being met and the political corruption that kept such inequity in place. The Skid Row I witnessed is just one of endless examples of fundamental needs not being met for myriad populations in the United States, due in part to marginalization of the poor and people of color.

I became aware at a young age of the systemic racism and classism in my culture and my own privilege, from my parents, who originally met as social workers. My family was steeped in service, and my parents at times took vulnerable children into our own modest home to live. I understood that the majority of people who were homeless or marginally housed had not failed the system but had been terribly failed *by* the system. Often, within Los Angeles, entire families became homeless overnight due to a myriad of scattered and hard-to-access social services that failed to provide a safety net during times of need. While popular culture demonized homelessness as the failure of dysfunctional people and the mentally ill, this could not have been further from the truth.

At the beginning, my mom worked primarily with undocumented immigrant families from Mexico and Central America. By the 1980s, she was working almost exclusively with homeless families, the majority Black single parent households from South Los Angeles. My mom was the person people called when they had nowhere to turn to: no resources, no roof over their head, not a dime. Her work was about creative strategies for long-term solutions for families to feel supported in turning their lives around. I witnessed the power of one human being committed to innovating positive social change. I experienced the beauty of a community of ordinary people coming together to be of service. But I also witnessed the horrifying bureaucracy and painful losses. Feeling helpless, there was a time when I chose to "turn down the volume" on the oppression I witnessed because it felt too overwhelming. The paradox of my own privilege within this paradigm felt continually confusing.

Yet the world around us in Los Angeles seemed to continue to operate as if nothing were wrong. It seemed as if we were supposed to accept inequity as a fact of life. Although these feelings infuriated me to the core, I did not know what to do with that fury other than participate in my mother's dedicated efforts the best I could and commit to leading a life of service.

There was far too great a contrast between the pain I witnessed and felt and the "keep smiling" attitude of our community. "Keep it light" and "have fun," as well as "be strong" and "compete," were the prevalent messages in my social circle, and I found this cultivation of denial and sunshining deeply perplexing. I was overwhelmed by the paradox between the painful realities I witnessed and experienced and the social focus on "positivity." Over the years, I came to understand this as a very common experience of adolescence. While everyone's experience of inner turmoil is different, there is something collectively traumatic about the culture of denial of real-life experiences.

The Heart Embraces Everything: Beyond the Duality of Positivity versus Negativity

Consider the collective social agreement held in many social circles to remain positive. While there is nothing intrinsically wrong with positivity, it affirms duality and promotes the belief that the alternative is negativity. In other words, there is either a positive state of being or a negative state of being. This approach to life rejects that place in our hearts that has room to welcome the full spectrum of positive to negative experiences. Far too often, in times of pain or grief or when navigating difficult emotions, we receive the message to negate the bad feelings to free ourselves from them. The messages we receive from the dominant culture are repetitive:

Lighten up. Get over it.
Stay positive.
Look on the bright side of things.
Smile and be happy.
Cheer up . . . this will make you feel better.
Don't be a downer. Find the silver lining.
Don't burden anyone with your problems.
Remember all you have to be grateful for.

To reject one half of the human experience has become a cultural and societal norm. This focus on "feeling better," "staying positive," and *negating* pain, anxiety, distress, grief, or disappointment is rarely questioned. It has stunted our collective emotional intelligence and given birth to a multibillion-dollar pharmaceutical industry, along with endless self-help schemes that do not address the primary source of human suffering.

Positivity is not bad. It's just deeply limited. Sometimes positivity gets misused to justify closing our hearts to our human experience. We sometimes judge ourselves or others for not being positive. We justify turning away from discrimination in our world where we could be of service. The constant effort to stay positive can keep us locked in binary perception, limiting our capacity for authentic joy. In other words, by trying to focus on the positive we maintain the negative in our awareness continually.

For me, sunshining fostered the belief that there was something wrong with me for not feeling upbeat all of the time. My attempts to achieve a threshold of what happiness should look like prevented me from recognizing the gift of my own unique and multidimensional self. I later learned, through my practice, that an even deeper and more vibrant joy than I had ever imagined is available when we release the duality of positive versus negative and meet all of life with the love of our open heart.

Positivity is the sister to rationality. They are two poles, holding up the dualistic expectation of hierarchical perception, encouraging people equally to cut off their intuition and emotions. The following are examples of messages we often hear:

- Be logical.
- Be reasonable.
- Don't be too sensitive.
- Be sensible.
- Your worth is in your intellect.
- Be competitively intelligent.
- Have an opinion to debate with at all times.
- Be even-keeled.

Through these messages, we learn to numb our sensitivity and our pain—for ourselves, for others, and for our world. We abandon our empathy, in a sense, by negating our multitude of feelings. Both positivity and rationality position us to tune out our emotional intelligence.

Before I committed to meditation practice, this habit of *pushing away* the difficult stuff, which seemed to keep popping back up no matter how hard I tried to push it down, was exhausting. I worked to maintain a positive self-image and was appreciated for being a "bright light," yet that light did not include the whole of me. My pain was kept secret instead of made sacred. There was a nagging assumption that my sensitivity was a failure and that something irreparably horrible would happen if I faced the emotional darkness I carried alongside my light.

Aware of both impermanence and the need for change in our world, I wanted to scream, "Wake up!" and it was this energy that called me to dharma practice. I was looking for a response to the world that fused together, in an integrated way, the urgency of addressing the social-ecological work needed with the recognition of love, impermanence, and interconnection as a way of life.

Softening Our Gaze and Seeing What Is

My first long immersion in Zen Buddhism took place at Green Gulch Farm, a traditional Soto Zen Buddhist center and residential community on the breathtaking peninsula of Muir Beach, California. At the age of twenty-four, I had the opportunity to dip my toes into formal Zen practice while working as a farm apprentice on their verdant seven-acre organic farm, which included raised beds, vegetables and herbs, fields, and flower gardens. I had been meditating daily and attending retreats since I was nineteen years old, but this was my first in-depth immersion. At a time when I needed to pause, recover from a broken heart, and seek clarity on my direction, I found a temporary resting place at Green Gulch Farm.

After graduating from college, I worked for a global nonprofit organization protecting biological and cultural diversity. This organization helped indigenous land-based peoples around the world protect themselves from and recover from the pressures of modernization and globalization. I was also engaged in urban gardening projects for low-income communities and permaculture design. I had been lucky enough to work for some of my activist heroes during this time but felt confused by the level of drama, finger-pointing, burnout, and self-righteousness within the world of change-making that I sometimes witnessed. I was seeking a form of activism that was effective but equally expressed relational intelligence. The indigenous cultures I studied and worked on behalf of—which included the Ladakhi peoples of Northern India and traditional Bhutanese peoples—seemed to embody an alternative to the overconsumptive and unsustainable way of life my culture modeled.

I sensed in Buddhism something wholesome, timeless, and deep. I was craving relief from the culture of sunshining and sought an understanding of life that went beyond my culture's dualistic paradigm. Although I didn't realize this until I began practicing Zen, I was also seeking an understanding of life that went beyond the human mind. My thirst was quenched at my first Zen immersion. While I had experienced other meditation retreats, primarily in the Vipassana tradition, my immediate experience of Zen at Green Gulch Farm was direct recognition of the depth, dignity, and simplicity of the practice.

At Green Gulch, we woke before dawn each morning and began meditation at 5:00 a.m. In the *zendo*, a Japanese-style meditation hall, I was instructed to relax my eyes in their sockets and rest my attention within, with my eyes open but receptive and passive, rather than active or focused. This darkening of my visual field invited my mind into quietude, contributing to a more subtle and sensitive quality of perception. Through the *soft gaze*, I felt my mind and body began to naturally synchronize and my awareness began to organically expand.

I was quite impressed by the disciplined rigor of Zen and the *roshi's* dharma talks that blew my mind open but went just beyond the grasp of understanding and the exquisite Japanese rituals that had been passed down for thousands of years, but it was the simple instruction to soften my gaze that most reshaped my orientation to life. My eyes, which had been used to looking outward to the conditioned world for standards to meet and validation for how I was meeting them, were now invited to soften and release that relationship to the external world.

Whereas we often actively use our eyes to take in and assess the external world, in meditation we step back to become aware of the lens through which we are perceiving. Whether our eyes are resting in a soft gaze or closed entirely, we allow the aperture of our attention to expand so that it is no longer one-pointed. By opening our perception lens to include awareness of the internal landscape (our own mind, body, emotions, and heart), while equally including the larger landscape of the world we inhabit, we rest in 360 degrees of awareness.

The orientation of separate self, which stands outside of life looking in—viewing the world as a subject looking at an object—dissolves. By *softening our gaze*, we can experience ourselves more deeply, within the fabric of life rather than separate from it.

Through learning to cultivate a *soft gaze*, whether I was in sitting meditation or practicing informally throughout my day, I was surprised to realize the degree to which attention follows the gaze of the eyes. Growing up in Los Angeles, a city dominated by artificial light, with cell phones and colorful billboards, shiny marketing ads and a culture of wealth overlapping deep poverty, there was a constant onslaught of activity demanding my visual attention. I was more easily distracted by the external world and visual perception than I had admitted to myself. My attention was often pulled upward and outward into the realm of external distraction. In other words, I was often not settled or anchored within my body but caught up in the stories of my mind. I had received praise for my intellect and good judgment, but nowhere in my schooling had I been taught to be fully present in my body, where I could access a deeper and wiser source of intelligence.

The soft gaze invited me into a refuge of stillness that existed beyond judgment and labels. In the twilight temple of meditation, there was permission to set aside the assumptions of my inner narrative. There was room to feel the deeper undercurrents of my experience. There was permission to see and know myself far beyond the limiting narrative and identity of "Eden."

Through this soft gaze I came to understand that awareness is the subtlest form of love. Without any doing required, awareness seemed to welcome me exactly as I was . . . and welcomed life exactly as it was.

Humanity Requires Both Darkness and Light

Humanity requires physical darkness and light. Physical light helps us to distinguish between things. We rely upon physical light to dissect details, label, and separate. We might use light to insert thread through a needle, measure dimensions, or perform complex surgery. A painter relies on light to fill in small strokes and detail, to choose colors, and to define three-dimensional shapes. A photographer's entire intricate craft is about literally capturing reflected light. We rely on artificial light to manage tremendous amounts of information and communication through our computer screens.

In today's world, however, we are so reliant on light—physically and metaphorically—that we forget how to quiet our distinguishing faculties. We forget how to perceive from a deeper, more relational and receptive center within. We forget our capacity to see life as it is . . . and let that life be.

In a world that emphasizes the domain of artificial light and external distraction, we can be easily seduced into the habit of labeling, dissecting, measuring, comparing, and forming opinions about everything. We can mistake our rational mind for our center of perception and lose sight of our internal and interdependent world. We can disconnect from our emotions and the rhythms of our bodies because we are so tuned in to Wi-Fi. We can fail to acknowledge the subtler unseen, invisible, sensed, and felt aspects of our experience. We can literally lose awareness of life beyond the bubble of our mind.

Tibetan Buddhism considers this the age of *Kaliyuga*, an age of great darkness. In this interpretation, Kaliyuga does not point to darkness as evil or the absence of light but as *tremendous distraction*. The prophecy speaks of this time in human history as the most distracted time humans have ever faced, one in which there is an unprecedented amount of means to distract ourselves. These range, of course, from the internet and social media to food, drink, or intoxication and fake news. This includes the consistent distraction of bright and artificially lit screens and the glamorization of busyness. What we distract ourselves from is our true nature.

At the same time, the opportunity of this day and age for healing and remembering is vibrant because it is so evident that our old paradigm is no longer working. The portal for healing is revealed when we remember who we are beyond the brightly illuminated world of distraction. What we gain from this remembrance is recognition of our sensitivity, our nonseparation from all of life, and our joyful responsibility to all of life.

We cannot restore a more compassionate world out there without learning to do so within. Through the soft gaze, I began to remember the consciousness that sees and welcomes life as it is. I remembered the compassionate awareness that could hold my grief and my joy with equal softness. The experience felt like reuniting with a receptive friend, content to spend time with me no matter what mood I was in. This friend didn't take me personally. This friend did not take interest in the drama of my inner narrative. This friend did not try to caretake me. Meditation offered a bridge I longed for between the warmth of my heart and all the tender places that hurt.

Relaxing the Armor of the Spiritual Warrior

After my time at Green Gulch, I attended a five-day silent Zen meditation retreat in the springtime, in the Blue Ridge Mountains of North Carolina. Here, an important interview with my first long-term Zen teacher took place. In the Zen tradition, an interview is a personal guidance session between student and teacher.

Every day on retreat, we practiced sitting, walking, and working meditation, with occasional group gatherings and interviews with the teacher. After a morning of sowing seeds and weeding the herb gardens, I was instructed to ring the bell outside the guidance room for an interview. I stood outside the door and waited nervously, pretending to be calm. I could feel my heart pounding with expectation and anticipation. When I heard the ring of the Guide's meditation bell inviting me in, I entered, bowed formally, and sat down in front of her in a cross-legged position. I felt both intimidated and excited to be in her steady, calm, expansive presence. She seemed solid as a rock to me, radiating both compassion and fearlessness.

She asked me, "What would you like to look at today?" And I replied sincerely and intensely, "I'm here to face the fire." I had been influenced by the notion of the spiritual warrior who will go to any end to awaken. The battle was between light and dark, love and fear, purity and delusion, consciousness and ego. I viewed spiritual practice as a way to transcend my difficulties and do away with the human ego, which was the demon at the core of all the world's problems. I was willing to walk through the primordial fire to achieve this. I believed that if I was rigorous and diligent enough, I could work my way to enlightenment.

The Guide invoked a pause before I could go into further explanation and looked back at me with a warm steadfast gaze that made me feel more relaxed about life than I had in a long time. After a lingering silence, the Guide responded in a calm, clear tone, "Where's the fire?" I immediately laughed and felt my entire body soften and settle with relief.

Although of few words, her response communicated a profound teaching about Zen. As I looked around, from the perspective of the present moment, I couldn't locate a fire. There was nothing actually going on but breath, body sensations, air touching my skin, and present-moment connection. It had never occurred to me that I was conditioned to equate achieving peace with exerting effort or battle to do so. Zen suggested that peace was already intact. It was not something to transcend my human self to get to but was instead something to *return to*. It was not something to attain one day when I fixed my messy human self. Wholeness existed here, in present-moment awareness. My job was to recognize this.

I became curious about my hypervigilant attempt to battle my demons and seek transcendence. I became more aware of the tendency to approach life through the archetype of the *yang*, active, intense, hardworking spiritual warrior and agent of change. I had been trying to get rid of my thoughts, dismember my ego, and work my way to spiritual understanding.

After that encounter, the armor of my internal warrior began to soften. Zen introduced me to the relaxed art of pausing, seeing clearly, and being present with what is.

While it's true that practice is not always easy, it is much easier than we've been conditioned to think. It is not the battle of the solo, heroic, masculine warrior of light against dark. It is a journey of soft surrender, relaxed attention, subtle awareness, and persistent kindness. Liberation requires wholehearted commitment, but awakening is a continual motion of opening to *embrace* rather than to *battle* life. It requires the ever-emerging courage that comes from the spirit of curiosity and discovery rather than force.

Everything about Zen felt counterintuitive to what I had been taught. From that point on, practice asked me to set aside the known and walk step-by-step into the unknown. Instead of holding a heroic torch of light, I was asked to move blindly into the dark. I could trust only my direct experience as a guide. Rather than relying on my intellect and mental effort, I was asked to surrender my constant striving and pay attention from a darker center of intelligence. I sensed the implication of this shift for me personally and for my capacity to be of service.

There is an old Zen proverb that states, "What was never lost can never be found." Rather than trying to get somewhere in practice, I began to allow each moment, as it already was, to invite me home. My pursuit of enlightenment expanded to include endarkenment.

* * *

MINDFUL INQUIRY

Have you ever been impacted by the culture of sunshining? Has there been a time in your life when you felt that part of your human experience was left out or diminished by the culture of sunshining? How did this feel? What was the impact on you?

Has the notion of the solo heroic spiritual warrior impacted your life or path of practice? Have you tried to battle shadows within you? Have you perhaps attempted to eliminate your ego through spiritual practice rather than embrace it? Or to be hypervigilant to try to attain enlightenment?

What is the equivalent for you of the twilight temple? The place, practice, person(s), or community that has supported you in remembering wholeness? That has helped to honor your pain and love for our world? Or that has helped you to release external and conditioned standards and simply be yourself?

* * *

EXPERIENTIAL PRACTICE: SOFT GAZE

Please allow yourself to sit in a comfortable position. Allow your eyes to rest open and relax your eyes in their sockets. Allow your eyes to be soft rather than focused or one-pointed. While we spend a lot of time actively using our eyes and assessing what we see, this is an inactive, passive, open, resting gaze. Notice the experience of the soft gaze on your entire being.

As you go about your day, please pause from time to time to soften your gaze. What do you notice?

* * *

EXPERIENTIAL PRACTICE: SOFT GAZE WALKING MEDITATION

Pick a place, either outdoors or indoors, to do walking meditation for at least ten minutes. If you are a wheelchair user, you can do this moving mindfully at an intentionally slow pace in your wheelchair.

Allow your eyes to rest in a soft gaze. Standing, bring awareness to your breath and your feet making contact with the ground beneath you. Take a moment to shift your weight back and forth to feel how this feels. Now begin to slowly walk, one step at a time, maintaining a soft gaze and feeling the contact between your feet and the earth below you. Move at a slow pace, with no agenda other than paying attention. As you walk, you can hold the intention, Going nowhere, doing nothing. *What do you notice?*

PART THREE

The Spiritual Teachings of Divine Darkness

The dominant paradigm assumes that the light, fast, active, and yang aspects of nature are superior to the dark, slow, receptive, and yin aspects. The following chapters in this part will invite you to explore the counterintuitive wisdom and spiritual teachings of darkness and the yin element of nature.

5

Seeing in the Dark

The Quiet Power of Receptivity

Darkness is not dark to God. The night is as bright as the day.

BARBARA BROWN TAYLOR[1]

ONE NIGHT DURING MY FIRST FEW MONTHS living as a monk, I was walking home to my hermitage much later than usual. It was springtime during the new moon, the lunar phase when we cannot see any moonlight whatsoever. I had planted a round of seeds for summer harvest that day and had given them a 10:00 p.m. watering after a community dharma meeting. I had been struggling with a tirelessly busy mind, which was, I suspected, a way of resisting the silence. On that night I felt exhausted by my inner narrative.

My flashlight died halfway to my hermitage, and I became more viscerally aware of the dense and pitch-black darkness of the night. I slowed down my pace in order to sense and feel my way through the obscure forest path with even more care. At first, I was cautious and even a little suspicious of the night surrounding me. And then my senses began to open, not just to a more attentive way of moving, which I was familiar with through the practice of *walking meditation*, but to something beyond my accustomed perception. I began to feel myself not walking *through* the darkness but *with* the darkness—completely dissolving into it.

Fascinated by what was happening, I sat down on the forest floor to meditate. My experience distilled to the simplicity of breath, earth, and darkness. My sense of Eden on her walk home, fatigued from the day's work and with an agenda of climbing into bed, dissipated completely. I became one with the divine darkness. An impeccable quiet descended, and I experienced my body as being infinite, extending out as endless space and time above, below, and around me. I remained sitting on the forest floor for an extended period of time, bathing in a bath of infinity.

I finally understood that my entire inner narrative was an effort to avoid this quality of surrender. Surrendering meant freedom within my heart and, I came to slowly realize, the death of my ego.

At that moment, I woke up to the benevolent spirit of physical darkness. I experienced that which is referred to by spiritual seekers as "the great void" as vibrantly alive, rather than a lonely or terrifying space. This subtle shift in consciousness changed my life forever and nourished the seed of endarkenment within.

Meditation is an invitation to bathe in darkened stillness. It is about taking refuge in the infinity from which everything arises and will return. *Infinitas*, the Latin root of the word *infinity*, means "without end." In darkened stillness, we can remember the consciousness that is without end. We can remember the state of being that is without boundaries.

This experience helped me to understand that my fear of darkness was in reality a fear of emptiness or nothingness. I have witnessed this fear in every person I have mentored at some point in the journey.

As we become present to the experience of darkness, we learn that darkness is not the "absence of something." Nor is emptiness. It is the *presence* of something, a *spaciousness*, a wild and loving field that welcomes everything. Shared consciousness. Nothing and no one left out.

The experience of meditating in the dark of the new moon signified a shift in my understanding of awakening. I realized that we do not meditate to attain an enlightened state. We meditate to remember the *already awakened state. It is through doing nothing but surrendering that we realize wholeness.* The next phase of my practice was about relearning the profound power of receptivity and surrender.

Waking Down: Shifting Your Center of Gravity

Your body already knows the way home. Your attention is the key that unlocks the door. The phrase *waking up* is often used in spiritual circles but *waking down* is more honest on the path to endarkenment. It is through *embodied presence*, rather than mental effort or philosophizing, that we remember the already awakened state. Eihei Dogen, the twelfth-century founder of Zen, referred to meditation as a "return to source."[2] There is a surprising simplicity to this practice, and it carries unrelenting depth. We learn to be aware of our physical body, our subtle energetic body, and the *field consciousness*, or shared body, of the world we inhabit. We practice living from source connection in every moment, thus remembering our home in the body of all beings. Thich Nhat Hanh refers to this as "interbeing."[3]

Meditation begins by finding a comfortable physical posture, typically upright, and relaxing mental effort. We *consciously allow* our body to be as it is. We *consciously allow* our breath, mind, and feelings, to be as they are. We *consciously allow* life to be as it is—without trying to fix, solve, change, improve, cling to, or resist anything. Body and mind can integrate organically when we pay relaxed attention and let ourselves be.

Conscious allowing can be a perplexing concept because the dominant paradigm has no reference point for this. Most of us have been conditioned to exert mental effort, control, and force to some degree in order to survive. Conscious allowing does not equate to laziness, apathy, or passivity. It does not require effort in the way of force or strain. The only effort is in paying attention to our present-moment experience through our natural awareness.

Many of us fill our lives with busyness at all times—if not in our bodies, then in our minds. Judging, assessing, and striving are all ways of filling, while meditation is about emptying. While discipline is required for meditation practice, the most important elements are actually the opposite of effort—*softening and letting go*. We give ourselves permission to empty out in order to remember life's already existing wholeness.

Yin and *yang*, *conscious allowing* and *conscious protection*, and dark and light exist in nature in sacred partnership. Thus, we also practice conscious protection in practice, alongside conscious allowing. We access conscious protection when we show up with discipline to meditate every day. It requires conscious protection to set boundaries with our own conditioned thoughts, and sometimes with other people's energy. In a relational conflict, conscious protection enables us to speak our truth with dignity, while conscious allowing enables us to listen and witness with nonjudgment. Conscious allowing supports us to pay attention to what is, while conscious protection enables us to choose a caring response. Through engaged meditation, we can learn to embody the balance of conscious allowing and conscious protection in everyday life.

*   *   *

EXPERIENTIAL PRACTICE: THE PRACTICE OF
CONSCIOUS ALLOWING AND DOING NOTHING

As you engage in this practice, set the intention to welcome your experience in the moment, as it is. Let go of labels such as good/bad, pleasant/unpleasant, right/wrong. If they arise, you can notice these labels and simply let them go.

Now take a few deep breaths and allow your breath to relax you.

As your breath returns to its natural rhythm, allow your breath to be as it is. Feel the weight and shape of your body supported by the surface and earth beneath you.

Now take five minutes or longer to practice doing nothing intentionally. Not trying to meditate. Not concentrating. Not planning. Not fixating on sensations you notice.

Let your body be as it is. Let your mind be as it is. Let life be as it is.

Consciously allow yourself to rest in the now.

If you notice effort or strain, give yourself permission to soften effort. Exert less effort.

What do you notice as you consciously do nothing? Perhaps you feel permission to fully let go. Perhaps you simultaneously feel the dissatisfaction of the part of you that doesn't want to be in the now. Take your time to rest and notice. Please make any notes you wish to make.

Receptivity Is an Expression of Respect for Life

Suzuki Roshi, when teaching dharma in Northern California in the 1960s and early 70s, was known to say to his students while they were in sitting meditation, "Express yourself fully."[4] It might sound ironic to address a group of silent meditators who are doing absolutely nothing but sitting still in *zazen* with this encouragement. He was pointing to the powerful expression of doing nothing but giving one's full attention to the moment. Through counterintuitive wisdom, Suzuki Roshi was pointing to *being* as an alternative to the active *doing* definition of expression. In a way, this teaching emphasizes receptivity as true nature expressing itself. Through receptivity, we begin to realize that the extraordinary power of our ordinary self requires no effort or strain.

Receptivity is a greatly overlooked and undervalued natural human quality. It is the still, dark, yin expression of nature. Receptivity is not the same thing as passivity. Receiving is an action, but it is relational. When we are receptive, we can take life or take another person into us.

Receptivity is our ability to listen to life as it is—without imposing our ideas or agendas onto it. This is not solely listening with our ears but with our whole body. Think of it as listening to energy, vibration, life force. Through receptivity, we live in a fully engaged and reciprocal conversation with life—attuned within and without at the same time.

Our bodies are an instrument for receptivity beyond what we can imagine, but in today's world, most people are not trained to tune or play this instrument. Although most of us associate the word *receptivity* with gentleness and softness, receptivity is actually a tremendous source of untapped power for humanity. It is the most important component of relational intelligence, love, and shared power, and we will explore it more in coming chapters.

Receptivity is an expression of respect for the world we inhabit.

Think of how you feel when someone truly listens to you without judging, offering their opinion, or trying to solve. Reflect on how connecting it feels when you are truly witnessed by another. Or when you receive the wordless sensory communication of the natural world around you. How does it feel when you listen to a piece of compelling music with your whole body and full undivided attention? Think of how it feels to slow down and enjoy the pleasure of your physical senses, without any agenda or distraction. Or when you rest in receptivity with a lover you trust, allowing erotic curiosity to guide you in pleasure and ecstasy.

If we are lucky, we experience the power of receptivity in our relationships with caring parents, healers, skillful mentors, and leaders. Yet it is more popular in today's world to meet one another through the expressive, imposing, or controlling aspects of our beings. We share our opinions, gossip, offer advice, judge one another, complain and *kvetch* to one another. We might appear to be listening to someone while being distracted by our own opinions or inner narrative. Few people give themselves and others the permission to coexist in quietude and relaxation in order to experience one another in a more receptive and generous way.

We exist in *relationship* in every moment of life. In every moment, there are multiple layers or dimensions of communication coexisting—within ourselves, with other human beings, with the natural world, and with the invisible realm. We cannot awaken from egocentricity or anthropocentricity without developing our receptivity. If we are not receptive, we miss out on the conversation life wants to engage in with us. Our primary relationship is limited instead to the self-referencing and self-absorbed conversation of our conditioned mind.

Receptivity Is a Path for Relational Intelligence

We develop our receptivity by anchoring in our bodies and practicing *deep listening*. *Deep listening* is a natural capacity. When we give our full attention to listening—within and out—the separate self dissolves. Every form of life on earth responds to the language of listening. Listening is an act of exercising the nonseparation that is our birthright.

An ancient Zen koan instructs, "Listen with your feet." A koan is not meant to be understood through the cognitive mind. If we bring receptive awareness directly into our feet, or into our entire bodies, we can open our minds and experience to a much broader expression of listening.

Deep listening is a yin strategy for being of service to life. After years of being part of a community of activists who focused solely on action, I learned experientially that receptivity in balance with action makes us much more skillful agents of change. An effective change agent understands that deep listening is the first step to collaboration. Collaboration is the first step to skillful action. By *collaboration*, I mean stepping aside from one's ego agenda and tuning in, instead, to *we consciousness*. *We consciousness* is the field of shared presence that takes us beyond an I-versus-you mentality. We consciousness does not negate difference or individuality. It is the spacious awareness that holds respectfully your personal experience alongside the many dimensions of whomever you are with. This field can hold with kindness and dignity difference, discomfort, and adversity. Rather than making life just about myself, my opinion, or what I want right now, we consciousness instead inquires *What is best for the whole in this moment?* When we attune to a group field instead of relying on our self-referencing mind, that field can inform us. And that field also includes us.

Through meeting uncomfortable, triggering conversations and situations with receptivity, I have learned that we consciousness is always available. There is a common invisible meeting ground that exists only in the present moment. When our differences feel vast and impenetrable, we can feel guided to cause less harm and instead show up in a more collaborative way.

As a white woman writing about we consciousness, it feels important for me to acknowledge humbly that this term is an antidote to the Western myth of separation. There are indigenous cultures on our planet today who do not even experience the I-versus-you mindset. It feels equally important to emphasize that this is not a pseudo-spiritual term that assumes all to be one while negating racial complexity and the reality of difference and individuality. We consciousness is an experience, in the moment, of recognizing oneness at the same time as difference.

My Personal Journey to Shared Power: Emptying Out in Order to See

It took me a long time to surrender to the power of receptivity. I had spent decades trying to meet the demands and expectations of a society that celebrated productivity, performance, competition, and extroversion. Although I considered myself to be highly empathic, I had been conditioned by the culture around me to undervalue and diminish the receptive or yin aspects of my nature. When I finally surrendered, it was as if I could not believe that my innate receptivity was actually my greatest gift. *Everything I had been seeking was already within me. I had just been looking in the wrong direction, seeking outward toward the sun instead of inward toward the moon.*

In the year 2000, I met one of the most influential teachers of my life. My Zen teacher recommended that I schedule a reading with a clairvoyant who channeled a Tibetan master named Ramada. It would be timely, she said, to seek a larger perspective on my karmic patterns over many lifetimes, as related to my work in this lifetime. The next chapter of my spiritual path was about reclaiming my body as an instrument of receptivity.

The first thing I noticed when he greeted me at the door of his unassuming center in Sacramento was that his gaze was more penetrating than anything I had ever experienced in my life. He did not look at me as a physical being, but as the multidimensional soul who had been circling the sun for ages. I felt him taking in the complexity of my entire being rather than my surface identity. He scanned my energetic system from the cellular level to the universal—my past, present, and future simultaneously. I could feel no judgment, no ego, and no agenda other than clear seeing as he took in the entirety of my being.

While impressed by his unusual and penetrating perception, it was his dry and eccentric sense of humor that allowed me to feel completely comfortable in his presence. I could tell that he had zero lines drawn between the mystical and the ordinary—no lines of like or dislike around anything he might see in me. He was free of duality. He welcomed the paradox of personality quirks alongside the timeless nature of the soul.

In our first session, I felt self-conscious under his gaze, but his unwavering acceptance helped me to see myself without any judgment. There was no hiding my shadows, my weaknesses, my irrational fears, my Virgo perfectionism, my perceived failures or imperfections in his presence. There was nowhere to hide. Seeing him see into me with nothing but love taught me how to see myself with pure love.

Our conversations over the next fifteen years of my life, until he passed away from cancer, transformed me. They brought clarity to intricate and complex aspects of personal growth as well as to collective consciousness. Ramada was a proponent of self-teaching. We are our own best teachers. If we practice simply observing the patterns of our life and cultivating compassionate awareness, we can each access the answers and truths that we need. This directly correlated to Zen, in which realization occurs through direct embodied experience.

Ramada encouraged in me the clear perception that many wisdom traditions refer to as "seeing in the dark." In our first conversation, he suggested that I could go no further until I let my belief center open completely. I had learned to rely on my intellect and belief center devotedly to survive a world that overvalued intellect. He suggested that my existing assumptions needed to be let go entirely in order to open to a deeper source of knowing and not knowing. My beliefs needed to be emptied to make space for fresh insight into the nature of things, beyond assumptions I had always held as true.

It takes courage to perceive through our heart, rather than visual-cognitive-rational perception—and to accept what we see. Consider that metaphorically, human beings only have the capacity to visually see certain parts of the spectrum of light. We do not see all parts of the light spectrum that are available to many animal species and insects. We see a limited spectrum and assume it to be the full spectrum. We are able to see, however, the full spectrum of darkness.

I realized firsthand that only when we cease holding tightly to old beliefs and the continually discriminating mind is there space for completely new information. Through self-observation, I realized that much of the time we see or hear only that which we want to see or hear. We subconsciously block out all types of information that do not fit our conditioned paradigm or self-perception. As a quote attributed to Ken Wilber states, "Most of us are only willing to call 5 percent of our present information into question at any one point."[5] The point of meditation is not to replace our old beliefs with new ones but to access the perception that is free of beliefs.

We also limit our perception on a daily basis because we do not want to see or experience that which we label as "dark." We try to hide shadows within ourselves in order to be seen in a certain light. The reality is that the brightest lights often cast the biggest shadows. We can embrace the paradoxes of existence—or we can close our eyes and see only what we want to see.

Under Ramada's mentoring, I began to empty my mind and shed limiting beliefs that I had held for my entire life. I began to let my body guide me with greater conviction. I honored my intuition with greater certainty. I celebrated, rather than discounted, the constant connection I felt with the invisible realm, seeing myself in a completely different light. This capacity for inner vision felt like uncovering a simple treasure, buried by the ancients, that modern civilization had somehow overlooked. There was no egoic sense of owning the insights or information that came to me. Rather, there was a humble recognition that insights arise from field consciousness—and that it was my joy and responsibility to live in the openness in which I was available to receive them.

As part of his teaching on *emptying*, Ramada shared the shamanic wisdom of *becoming like a hollow bone*. *Hollow bone*, originally an indigenous Lakota teaching, suggests that it is only when we allow ourselves to empty completely, letting our body-minds become like a hollow bone, that we make ourselves available to be vessels for spirit. This teaching emphasized by every shamanic teacher I have had can be thought of as learning to rest in receptivity. We allow our body to become like a hollow bone and act as a conduit and channel for deep listening.[6]

Receptivity, contemplation, empathy, and attunement had always been part of the repertoire of my being. But these yin personality traits were not valued, nor were they celebrated by the dominant paradigm. I had at times been embarrassed by the level of sensitivity I seemed to carry within. I was cautious with whom I shared certain experiences, knowing that this kind of sensitivity was often judged. I had worn a protective shield around my nature, and Ramada helped me to finally embrace it.

Sister to hollow bone is the Zen concept of meeting everything in life with a *beginner's mind*. When we meet each moment with a *beginner's mind*, we meet life with the wonder and openness of a child. We meet life empty and open rather than full. We can think of beginner's mind as "original consciousness." This can be compared to a childlike innocence, but it is not naive. It is here that we are free to receive life. Suzuki Roshi taught that "In the *beginner's mind* there are many possibilities, but in the mind of the expert there are few."[7]

From a beginner's mind there is room to welcome new information—including information that is outside of our awareness. From a beginner's mind we allow direct experience to be our guide. A beginner's mind invites us to shift from egoic confidence or control to openness and vulnerability. Although we typically equate the expert with strength, it is the beginner who carries the ultimate strength. The fool, rather than the expert, is available for collaboration with life.

Both Zen and shamanism emphasize the patience and perseverance required to fine-tune one's instrument for receptivity. A hollow bone does not become hollow overnight. It might sit out in the desert sun decaying for years, under the forces of nature and the passage of days and nights. Likewise, cultivating genuine emptiness through spiritual practice can take time and the willingness to become seasoned.

Receptivity Modeled by Nature: Incubation as Power

Receptivity is magnetic. Consider Mother Earth herself—a prime example of receptivity. The Earth is not solely a mass of rock and water moving through space. She is an all-powerful magnetic force with a North Pole and South Pole, holding together the atmosphere, the oceans, and all expressions of life. She is the unified field of *Gaia consciousness*, living in constant emergence, adaptation, communication, and collaboration.

Receptivity invites life into unity. In receptive stillness we can welcome the complex and contradictory aspects of our human experience into a unified field. A skillful leader can nourish unity within a diverse group by simply holding conversations, conflicts, and emotions in a nonjudgmental way. A facilitator who understands the value of receptivity can allow the myriad opinions and needs of a diverse group of people to coexist rather than emphasizing division. This facilitator is not actually creating unity but, rather, nourishing the circumstances for the backdrop of unity to be revealed instead of feeding separation.

Receptivity is the path of *authentic power*. Power is not something we speak about much in Buddhism, but authentic power is what we reclaim through embodying receptivity. *Authentic power* is the ability to give and receive love in every moment. While giving and receiving love in every moment might sound ambitious, love begins with paying attention. *Are we paying devoted attention within our self? Are we paying full attention while engaging with one another?* Authentic power, which we will explore further in chapter 8, is the expression of shared power or power *with* rather than power *over*. Shared power is not a fixed state we arrive to but a continual conversation and awareness practice. Through the quality with which we pay attention, we affirm our undeniable recognition of the interconnection that is who we are. We can learn the value of meeting life from the shared strength of an unguarded heart.

In the words of David Hawkins, the renowned psychiatrist, physician, and spiritual teacher, "For our purposes, it is really only necessary to recognize that power is that which makes you go strong, while force makes you go weak. Love, compassion, and forgiveness, which may be mistakenly seen by some as submissive, are, in fact, profoundly empowering."[8]

Genuine power is anchored in interconnection rather than identification with the separate isolated self. It comes from knowing ourselves as part of the connective tissue or mycelial network of life. When we perceive ourselves as separate, we might try to show up appearing strong, impressive, defensive, or competitive. From shared power we understand that showing up as we are—in honesty, vulnerability, and authenticity—is power. Our power lies in our willingness to be human together, to stay present, and to move beyond the conditioned manuals we have been given.

Authentic self or true nature is sometimes referred to as "no self" in Zen. It is what remains, for each and every one of us, when our preoccupation with identity is released and we allow life to animate us.

Power Rather Than Force

The culture of capitalism emphasizes productivity, individuality, and force. It emphasizes ways of being that keep the myth of separation in place. Consider some of these messages that are woven into the dominant paradigm. Consider, with compassion, how they may be alive in your own psyche:

Force is more effective than gentleness.
One needs to be aggressive in this competitive world.
One needs to perform at one's best constantly.
If you are quiet, you will be overlooked. One's opinion needs to be heard in every matter.
There is no time to listen. There is something that needs to get done.
Bigger is better. More is better. Faster is better. Louder is better.

Humanity is in the early stages of correcting these biases in so many domains of life where force and action are considered more powerful than *receptivity*. For decades science has emphasized the primary value of the sperm in the fertilization of the egg in human procreation. It was assumed for a long time that whichever sperm actively penetrated the passive inert egg most quickly won the race to victory. In recent years, however, there is a dawning awareness that reproduction is not solely based on the active surging competitive nature of the sperm cells. In fact, the passive egg determines to a much larger extent the process of reproduction. If the egg is not receptive, the sperm is rejected.

Likewise, conventional obstetricians have assumed for decades that force is required for the birthing process itself. Midwifery, which is regaining popularity, is an art of conscious allowing. Midwifery recognizes that it is natural for the female body to know how to give birth. By doing less and attuning to the body's organic process, we can support nature to take its course. In the words of the writer and birth activist Sheila Stubbs, "The midwife considers the miracle of childbirth as normal and leaves it alone unless there's trouble. The obstetrician normally sees childbirth as trouble; if he leaves it alone, it's a miracle."[9]

The wisdom of "less is more" is modeled in many nonviolent strategies for engaging skillfully with life without causing harm to it. These strategies include the following:

- Regenerative agriculture, which understands the importance of the "no till" method for global topsoil building and for healing the global crisis of climate change.
- Sustainable design, in which the intention is less input and energy for greater impact, thus conserving global resources and honoring ecological relationships.
- Somatic therapy, a healing modality that acknowledges the body's innate capacity to guide its own process for healing trauma when we apply deep listening and allow it to do so.
- Yin yoga, a conscious movement practice that recognizes the restorative power and impact on our bodies of slowing down and honoring the receptive rather than active aspect of our being.
- Tai chi and qigong, ancient martial arts disciplines for achieving greater outcome from less effort, which is a core principle of sustainability and regeneration.

* * *

MINDFUL INQUIRY

Think of someone who deeply listens to you, someone in whose presence you feel truly seen and heard. How does it feel to be in this person's presence? What are the qualities of this person's presence?

How have you experienced the power of less is more? How have you experienced the efficacy of conscious allowing over force? Is there any aspect of your life today in which a less-is-more attitude might be helpful or help you to go beyond conditioning?

*   *   *

EXPERIENTIAL PRACTICE: DEEP LISTENING

Deep listening is a meditative practice that we can continue to develop for the rest of our lives. Whether you are experienced in meditation or new to it, beginner's mind is the most helpful attitude to bring. If you are a deaf person, you can practice deep listening using sign language, paying attention with your whole body and resting in your receptivity.

You will need a partner so that you can take turns listening to each other. The person who is going to share first can choose any topic they could use support with.

Set a timer for ten minutes. Begin by pausing to each take in a few deep breaths, allowing the body to relax. Connect with the qualities of openness and curiosity. The listener will set the intention to give full relaxed attention to listening. Just like the breath is sometimes used as an anchor in meditation, listening is the anchor in this practice. Practice listening with your whole body. There is nothing to do but receive the other person's voice, words, and body language. You will also receive the energy and emotions behind the words. If you are practicing deep listening through sign language, pay attention to the energetics of the movements and shapes your partner signs in as well as the expressions on their face.

If mind commentary arises at any time, just notice it and gently but firmly return to listening. Allow whatever distraction arises to deepen your self-awareness. Does self-consciousness arise? Judgment? A desire to get listening "right"?

How does it feel to listen in an embodied present way? How does it feel to be listened to, without the other person inserting their opinion or offering advice?

EXPERIENTIAL PRACTICE: LISTENING TO MUSIC IN THE DARK

Choose some music that you find compelling. Turn off the lights or put on a blindfold. Relax your body and allow yourself to deeply listen, in the dark. Listen with your whole body, imagining that every cell in your body is receiving the sounds and rhythms of the music. How does it feel to listen to music without the stimulation of light through your eyelids? What do you notice?

*   *   *

EXPERIENTIAL PRACTICE: LISTENING TO A TREE

Take at least fifteen minutes for this practice. Step outdoors and allow yourself to be drawn to a tree that you can sit quietly and comfortably by. If you are someone who is homebound, you are welcome to do this practice with a houseplant. If the idea of tuning in to a tree/plant is outside the box for you, please practice beginner's mind. A tree/plant is an intelligent living being. First, greet this tree either with words or by offering your respect energetically. Close your eyes or put on a blindfold. Practice deep listening to this form of life. Let go of any agenda or expectation. Once you have listened for a while, you might ask a question about something you are seeking guidance on from this tree or plant. You might receive information through words, metaphor, images, or a feeling in your body. Just be open to receiving. What do you notice?

6

The Slow, Dark Processes

Healing and the Body

Between the head and feet of any given person
is a billion miles of unexplored wilderness.

GABRIELLE ROTH[1]

EARLY ONE WINTER MORNING AT the age of thirty-one, I woke up at my
hermitage in the woods feeling like I was in the body of a ninety-year-
old woman. A storm had come through during the night, wiping out a
baseline of physical well-being I had always known and cherished. What
remained was a degree of exhaustion, fogginess, and muscular inflamma-
tion that I had never before experienced nor imagined. I stumbled out of
bed and started a fire in my wood stove. I moved tentatively, evaluating
the foreign landscape of my body. I then began to slowly walk the forest
path to morning meditation.

That day began a long journey of diagnoses and misdiagnoses. No doctor could give me an explanation for my symptoms, though they eagerly

attempted to. It was not until over a decade later that I finally learned that I had Lyme disease from a tick bite that had gone undetected.

As I navigated the unfamiliar territory of compromised health, I would sometimes enjoy periods of well-being and temporary relief. This would be followed by a flare-up of overwhelming symptoms. There seemed to be no rhyme or reason to the ever-changing climate of my body. My prior sense of physical well-being was decimated.

Those who have navigated chronic and/or mysterious illness or borne witness to a loved one's journey through sickness know how icily sobering the experience can be. When the privilege or expectation of health is suddenly taken away, one is challenged to the core physically, mentally, emotionally, psychologically, and spiritually. There was no explanation nor reliable prescription for healing. Riding the destabilizing roller coaster of illness, internal stories began to churn about my future, my life, my worth, and my capability:

> *What if I don't heal? Will I still be a contribution to the monastery? To society?*
> *What if I don't have the energy to take care of myself? Or even survive in this world?*
> *What about the dreams I hold?*
> *Why is this happening to me?*
> *What have I done wrong to have invited this ominous illness into my life?*

There was a wordless fear that this illness made me less lovable. There was also a subconscious belief that good people didn't get sick to this degree. I must have done something terribly wrong to manifest this.

While the internal sirens of my conditioned mind screamed loudly, I was able to recognize the fear-based nature of the response. My training had prepared me well for adversity, and I could recognize FEAR as False Evidence Appearing Real. Though I would never consciously have chosen the experience of compromised health, I could choose to meet my experience with love and fierce compassion. This choice was a point of liberation and empowerment that has remained with me throughout my life.

Whether facing physical pain, disappointment, heartbreak, loss, and even the heart-wrenching reality of global uncertainty, we can learn to meet every experience with love rather than fear. We can remain open to the spiritual dimensions and life instructions encoded within our experience, rather than feed the limiting narrative of our minds.

Inquiry became my guide more than ever, and my fearful stories changed to questions based on love:

> *How can I meet this experience with an open heart and clear mind?*
> *What conditioning is being revealed that I now choose to let go of?*
> *What is my actual lived experience, moment by moment, when I release*
>   *the stories created by mind and emotion?*
> *If love is my ultimate purpose here, how can I remember love right now?*
> *How is this, too, a teacher of love?*

These questions could not be answered intellectually. My job was to allow each alchemical question to incubate within my body and to listen. Day by day, even as I struggled with physical pain, emotional dysregulation, and mental haziness, I inquired and listened for guidance. Sometimes immediate guidance arose, and sometimes I was required to rest in not knowing, which in itself brought more spaciousness to my experience.

There is a teaching in Zen to "*practice like your hair is on fire.*" I felt life asking me to take greater responsibility for the power of my mind than I ever had before. The refuge of *present-moment awareness* was my lifeline amid struggle. This was a still dark resting place that existed within my physical body yet extended far beyond it.

Awakening Subtle Body Awareness

It is popular in today's world to live somewhat disconnected from our physical body. Many people notice, upon coming to meditation, that their thinking mind has become their center of gravity. People often initially approach meditation as a mental exercise before genuinely experiencing the integration of body-heart-mind. It can be vulnerable to connect with and feel our bodies. Our bodies carry not only our joy to be alive, but all of our unhealed pain and historical trauma. Our history and level of ancestral trauma can greatly determine the degree to which we feel safe to connect with our own bodies.

When we pay attention to our body beyond the physical labels we habitually use, as a living field of energy, we encounter the subtle body. Think of the subtle body as the energetic layer of embodiment we feel and experience as the all-over aliveness of the body-mind. Practicing *subtle body awareness* grounds us more deeply in the now. Subtle body awareness guides us in navigating life viscerally and intuitively, through our felt sense. While Western philosophy tends to view the body and mind as separate, Taoism, Hinduism, and Buddhism all recognize the body as being neither solely physical nor solely spiritual but a fully integrated energy system.

Cultivating subtle body awareness is necessary to evolving a more caring, attuned, and awake relationship with ourselves, and I believe that it is key for navigating illness and healing within the body-mind. Every illness has an energetic, emotional, and spiritual component.

Conventional Western medicine often encourages us to view body and mind in duality. It often seeks to treat separate symptoms or parts without recognizing the energetic system as a whole. Many of the illnesses gaining momentum in our world today—environmental illnesses, trauma-based illnesses, autoimmune diseases, new degrees of sensitivities, and viruses—have presented challenges that cannot solely be met through treating the symptoms.

Slowing down to sense our bodies, thoughts, and emotions as energy changes how we relate to them. We don't have to take energy personally, but we can meet energy with kindness and respect. Rather than mentally trying to understand, fix, or solve the cause of a headache or the pain in our neck, we can rest in subtle body awareness and listen with curiosity to the energy itself. We can converse in our body's language as an expression of partnership with nature. In my experience, our body's capacity for healing is far greater than we have been conditioned to believe. If we take time to truly listen, setting aside our concepts and ideas and resting in stillness, our bodies can give us direct information about exactly how to take care of ourselves.

The energy of our bodies might speak to us through sensation, vibration, shape, temperature, or rhythm. It might speak to us through movement, image, color, symbols, or metaphor. We might listen to a particular sensation or emotion as energy and inquire, *What is my felt experience of the colors, textures, temperature, and emotions this energy carries? What is the shape it takes within my body? How do I experience this energy when I don't resist it or take it personally? And how does this energy respond to being witnessed and listened to? When I stop trying to understand it and simply observe, what happens? Is there a message contained within this energy? How can I meet this, too, with love?*

As I listened more deeply through subtle body awareness, I learned to be with painful sensations with a quality of gentleness that often allowed the pain to soften. I learned to bring fascination to the energetic experience I labeled exhaustion, which as a result enlivened my overall vitality. When I felt despair about being sick, I learned to sink deep down into the stillness beneath despair, and to thus meet the despair with caring acceptance. Practicing subtle body awareness became a path for meeting everything I was going through with compassionate presence.

The key, for me, was acknowledging and honoring the energy beyond my symptoms and stories. Instead of worrying or trying to solve the pain and fatigue that consumed my body, Lyme became a meditation: *What is happening right now? How am I relating to it? What is essential for me to give my energy to?* When we conserve energy that has been directed to anxiety and stress, we realize that we have exactly the energy we need for what is essential. While still living at the monastery, for example, I did not have the mental or physical energy for performing certain physical activities, tracking mental details, or completing linear tasks. Later, when I was living back out in the world, I often lacked the energy for socializing, networking, administrative work, and even reading. By then, however, I had learned to inquire, *What is of essence?* I learned that life always seemed to provide me with the energy I needed to meet the essentials. I was reminded that kindness, interconnection, and subtle body awareness were the most important essentials, no matter what. I was always provided the energy to meet life—internally and externally—with love. This helped to confirm that what I was made up of and could count on no matter what was love.

Lyme disease forced me to slow down and disable a habitual overproductivity. It enabled me to embrace the slow, dark processes of my nature ever more fully. By it disallowing me to engage with the energy level I had previously experienced, I had no choice but to sink down even more deeply into my spiritual practice. I felt night and day being turned upside down. In other words, my productive daytime self was paralyzed, but my nighttime self was empowered. While we cannot visually see the immediate benefits or results of gestating, incubating, resting, integrating, just being, and dreaming, they become obvious to anyone on the path of awakening.

I also learned that energy is never fixed and is always transmutable when applied to the subtle body. One morning, when I woke up from only three hours of sleep feeling particularly weak and in despair about my illness, intuitively I invited my despair and weakness into a dance. I turned on music, which was gentle at first, and then gave my body permission to move as slowly and freely as it wanted to. I began on the floor and let my subtle body energy take exactly the shapes it needed to. I invited my fatigue to express itself, my sadness to vibrate, and my fear to take shape through physical expression. I mentally got out of the way and let my body shake, flow, stretch, unfurl, and slowly reclaim the energy that was being held down by despair. Forty-five minutes later, my slow heavy dance had evolved and morphed into a fiercely energetic dance of ecstasy, vitality, and resiliency. I emerged in a state of empowerment and regeneration, hardly believing what had happened to me. From that day forth, dancing from my subtle body became a devoted part of my healing practice.

Through stillness, movement, and subtle body awareness, a spiritual empowerment began where I found myself becoming more settled and more somatically integrated. There are many definitions of love in the English language, my native tongue. An expression of love that is often left out or overlooked is *permission*. When we give our energy or life force absolute permission to express itself as it needs to, without any interference, we bring that energy into love.

Pathways to Inner Connection and Interconnection

Awakening occurs through direct experience in the present moment. There is also an awakening that is cultivated over time by refining our pathways of subtle body awareness. We expand our *inner awareness* and *nonlocal awareness. This is how our capacity for aligning our actions and choices with inner connection and interconnection grows.* Think of inner awareness as attunement to the internal landscape of our bodies, minds, and feelings. Through *awareness practice* we become more intimate with our physical body, our energetic subtle body, and our senses. We develop emotional awareness and awareness of our hearts and minds. We affirm inner connection, which informs our capacity to live in a compassionate relationship with ourselves. The more we are aware of the nuances of our internal experience, the more we can meet ourselves with love and *appropriate response.*

Nonlocal awareness affirms connection with the entire universe. It is our attunement to the world around us and the experience of knowing ourselves as part of the world. Nonlocal awareness includes the natural-world and spatial awareness, social and environmental awareness, and the shared human heart. This includes the nonhuman world, the invisible spiritual dimensions of life, and even awareness of other parts of planet Earth. Nonlocal awareness is the Gaia consciousness of life on planet Earth.

In the words of the writer Donna Goddard, "Extrasensory abilities are naturally developed within us by being more receptive to the subtler and finer messages around us. We all have extrasensory, as well as sensory, faculties."[2]

We do not need to fetishize nonlocal awareness. We do not need to label what we become aware of. What is significant about nonlocal awareness is remembering ourselves as part of the vast and wordless field consciousness, which releases us completely from the bubble of separate self. In meditation, we rest in 350-degree awareness, aware of the inner and outer dissolving, aware of awareness itself.

Joanna Macy speaks brilliantly to this when she acknowledges, "What I am, as systems theorists have helped me to see, is a 'flow-through.' I am a flow through of matter, energy, and information. The learnings I have digested from my life experience have been woven into this flow-through by both positive and negative feedback loops in the relationships of my life."[3]

The Regenerative Body of the Dark Earth

Healing requires us to meet our bodies as the mystery—with awe and reverence. While there is great emphasis in spiritual circles today on the *light body*, the light body concept encourages us to reach away from physical form to attain purity of the mind. The light body is painted as pristine, with rays of love and sunlight radiating outward. It is upheld as a spiritual standard, mimicking our idealized hierarchical standards of beauty and spiritual attainment. It perpetuates an attempt to purify the "impure human body" through cleansing, discipline, or rituals of intoxication. This bias toward the light body has roots in spiritual teachings ranging from Judeo-Christian theology to New Age spirituality and theosophy. The notion of pure versus impure feeds the false perception that there is something impeding our already existing wholeness. It encourages us to wage battle against impurity.

When we embrace our *earthly body*, the intention is not to purify. There is no hierarchy of pure versus impure on planet Earth. All forms of life belong equally and exist in symbiotic relationship. Nothing exists in isolation. Therefore, we might think of our earthly body as the symbiotic relationships, complexity, poetry, multidimensionality, and diversity of life energy expressed through our flesh and bones.

We might also remember that we share our earthly bodies with many forms of life, ranging from bacteria to fungi, viruses to archaea. The human body contains, in fact, ten times more microbes than cells.[4] When we fail to recognize the wisdom, beauty, and diversity of our earthly body, we miss out on the opportunity to cultivate healthy relationships and balance within our bodies.

In my experience of healing Lyme, it would have been misguided to wage war on the Lyme spirochete. I could not have done so without causing harm to the microbiome of my body—and harm to my sensitive heart. It never occurred to me that I somehow needed to be purified to become whole. What was helpful was to meet with respect and reverence the entire circle of symbiotic relationships existing within my body, including those with Lyme spirochete, fungi, protozoans, and viruses. This entailed cultivating a healthy and wildly diverse microbiome and accepting every organism in my body with love, rather than with negativity. Just as I recognized the sacred relationships within the soil of the gardens I stewarded, I embraced the microbial relationships and systems within my own earthly body.

Everybody has their own unique path, and every one of us has different needs and approaches to healing. Allopathic medicine can be a vital part of one's journey and can be lifesaving. It is my hope, however, that through the balance of light and dark, our world will continue to develop healing combinations of both traditional and allopathic medicines.

Like dark matter, perhaps the earthly body cannot be understood entirely by science. Our bodies are not just the physical. They are also the energetic, emotive, and mythical wilderness that is both uniquely ours and intricately connected to *Gaia* consciousness. Each of our bodies carries an intricate map of our ancestral history, cellular memory, and relationships that stretch beyond time and space.

Our bodies are our feedback system for all of life on planet Earth and change constantly, throughout each day, season, year, and our entire life span. The battle wounds and casualties of a hierarchical world are held within our bodies. The body will tell us who has been left out, where we are repressed, where we've become stagnant or weighed down by habit. The body will let us know where we are obeying other people's truths instead of our own. The body will show us what unlocks our zest for life and what nourishes our joy. The body will show us where we are holding back from a deeper power. Our earthly body reveals to us our past traumas, repressed feelings, and emotional baggage along with the mental baggage of dogmas, the inertia of self-doubt, and the dreams that have been discounted. Our bodies require love and compassion, and I'm not sure science has this piece down yet.

The gift of knowing darkness is the gift of knowing more of ourselves.

Healing the Body-Spirit Divide

Every *ism* we face today stems from a disconnect from our bodies and the natural world. Historically, the Cartesian era, Industrial Revolution, and capitalism reshaped human perception of the natural world and of our bodies into a paradigm based on logic, intellect, control, and consumption, and this body-spirit divide exists in many religions today, including Islam, Hinduism, and Christianity.

Buddhism is not immune to duality. The intersubjective nature of conditioning often keeps us from recognizing duality in the places where we least expect it. While it is not a rule that body and spirit are always separated in monastic training, I have witnessed the evidence of this divide within myriad monasteries and spiritual training centers.

Although it was a great privilege to live in a spiritual community, the monastery was not liberated from certain biases. The monastery operated with a rigorous schedule and a very strict formal hierarchical structure. To become a monk, one gave up one's entire life to practice in a concentrated way.

Monks were required to seek guidance from those higher up about every personal need that arose. When a monk had a personal or physical need, one first investigated the motivation behind the need. Is this an ego-driven need or a genuine need? If it felt genuine, one would post their request on the note board. The head monk would receive the note and seek guidance within or from the teacher. Sometimes a monk would receive a note in response. Sometimes the response was a spiritual instruction: "Let this go" or "Sit with this" or "Please investigate this assumed need more deeply." Sometimes a lack of response was the message in itself.

In an individualistic world, there is profound value in the kind of training that requires one to thoroughly investigate *what I want or think I need right now*. At times this system of minimal communication and the deemphasis on personal needs was liberating. At other times this system failed entirely. Ego/conditioning was pitted against true nature in a way that sometimes blurred the essence of practice. The overemphasis on keeping one's ego in check sometimes impeded compassion and upheld the duality between light/dark.

Having woken up one morning with a large bite on my right leg and severe pain along with it, I sought guidance and was instructed to sit with it. I didn't feel so sure about this, but my job as a monk was to obey guidance. Not until four days later, when I had a 103-degree fever and hallucinations was I permitted to go see a doctor. The doctor confirmed that I had been bitten by a black widow spider and that if I had waited one more day to come in, I could have lost my life. It took three weeks of bed rest and antibiotics to fully recover.

When my menstrual cycle ceased to flow inexplicably, I waited a few months before seeking guidance, to first investigate myself. When I finally posted a note, I received a response instructing me to sit with it. I posted a note about the same issue a couple of months later and received no response. In the end, I went three years without menstruating before a note I posted was finally responded to, and I was granted permission to see a doctor. When I finally saw a doctor, she was greatly alarmed about my condition and explained how it could endanger my bone health and entire endocrine system.

The doctor suggested that I needed to go on pharmaceuticals immediately, though this would only address the symptom. This was a profound wake-up call that perhaps the monastic power structure was not to be trusted over my inner guidance. I advocated instead to see a Taoist medicine qigong practitioner who lived far up one of the mountain roads near the monastery. When I arrived, she invited me to lie down on her healing table and rest. She spent the next forty-five minutes listening to my body with her subtly receptive hands. She did not lay her hands on me physically, but energetically, a couple of inches above my physical form. She asked my body if it wanted to heal and if it gave her permission. Then she told me to drive home and return in one week. Twenty minutes later, in the midst of my drive home, I began to bleed for the first time in three years. I cried tears of deep relief that my body knew how to come back to balance so easily. I vowed never to let my female body be discounted or dishonored again. My monthly cycle began that day in perfect continuity that has lasted since. Today I rest and engage in practices that honor my menstruation as a sacred ritual. I rest often in life today.

I realized sadly that I had allowed the hierarchical power structure of the monastery to undermine my kindred relationship with my own female body. I had let my devotion to the monastery distract me from letting the teachings be applied in the most relevant way. While the monastery's teachings spoke of empowering people to reclaim their internal authority, the power structure did not actually permit this. I had abided by the monastic hierarchy for so long that I had not yet seen the limitations of this structure. Only when I brought more awareness to hierarchy did my personal practice begin to mature and my physical healing begin to take root.

Through Lyme, I entered into the most confronting, courageous, and loving conversation with my body. *I learned to listen and speak in my body's native tongue.* I began to take responsibility for my own healing—in partnership with nature as my guide. While it does not serve to overidentify with, fixate on, or obsess about our bodies, to discount our bodies is to discount the seat of our authentic power. I believe that the degree to which we are willing to love and honor our physicality is equal to the degree to which we are willing to cherish nature's intelligence and receive nature's guidance. When we no longer recognize the sacred, sensual human body as divine, is this not an expression of a severe and dangerous disconnect from the living systems of planet Earth? I had traded in my ability to honor nature's guidance, through my own body, for a rigid concept of receiving guidance through hierarchy.

Surrendering to Slowing Down

Lyme was a great teacher of slowing down. When we let go of the insistence that going fast is more desirable than going slowly, we can allow our bodies to guide us in learning to balance attunement with productivity. There is nothing inherently wrong with slowing down. We might be less linear but become more intuitive. We might work less quickly but with more care.

Despite generations of conditioning from capitalism and marketplace mentality, our bodies know how to shift to the paradigm that values restoration and regeneration. *We can choose to slow down as a revolutionary act and learn to engage with life at our authentic pace.* We can choose to attune to our bodies rather than just using them as tools. We can recognize the first signs of depletion in ourselves and make a more conscious choice *in that moment.* We might notice our body quietly nudging us that it is time to pause . . .

slow down . . . or rest. We might also notice the subconscious motivation to keep going, to ignore our fatigue (mentally or physically) and push ourselves. We might notice a "grind it out" approach to our work. If we are observant, we might notice the initial moment that stress begins to build before we become overwhelmed. We might also notice the moment we shift from feeling present and fluid in our bodies to feeling rigid or constricted.

If the idea of slowing down evokes concern and even perhaps terror, I can assure you that opening ourselves up to the wisdom of the slower and darker aspects of nature does not lessen our productivity. By slowing down, we pay closer attention. We bring more care to everything we do. We are less likely to overlook an important detail. We find satisfaction in both the process and product of our work.

There is no benefit to continuing to pass down the imprint and patterning of depletion to our children. This ability to balance action with resting is vital to how we care for life.

Although there is nothing intrinsically good about the global COVID-19 pandemic, social scientists have reported a major shift among people at all income strata in the United States: They have rethought the pace of their prepandemic lives. Being forced to slow down helped many to recognize the impact the constant stress had on their bodies, lives, children, and general health and well-being. Lifestyle changes are not always possible, particularly at lower socioeconomic levels, but many people made changes they would have considered impossible just a year or so prior to the pandemic and subsequent quarantine mandates.

Turning Obstacles into Spiritual Opportunity without False Optimism

If our purpose here is love and liberation, everything that happens in life is a teacher of love and liberation. Our motivation becomes the benefit of all beings—including our ancestors that came before and future generations that will come after. Understanding our perceived obstacles as opportunities is not false optimism or *spiritual bypassing*. It does not mean that we should equate spiritual growth with difficult times. It does not mean that we avoid addressing the underlying dysfunctional systems that require our courageous attention. But we can open our hearts to seeing more clearly—with love—through difficult times. We can transform our relationship with the internalized conditioning that often controls our thoughts and actions during adversity.

Consciousness is not always pretty. Sometimes we have to face the fear that we will drown before we let go. Years later, I can say with certainty that Lyme disease was my greatest spiritual teacher. It shattered my sense of self and security rather brutally. At times, I wondered if I would survive. But it called upon all of me—more of me than I had previously brought into wholeness. It evoked a fresh understanding of love. It expanded my embodiment and expression of awakening dramatically, in ways I could not have foreseen.

While I acknowledge that not everyone recovers from Lyme disease, it was my experience with it that set me on a spiritual pilgrimage to facilitate the integration of my whole self. It was the unexpected bite of an arachnid that encouraged me, perhaps through destiny, to turn toward those parts of me that I had failed to recognize and celebrate. Having come to the other side of my journey in healing the Lyme disease that had attacked my body, I see Lyme as the dismemberment I had needed in order to make myself whole. There had previously been a rigidity and single focus in my Zen practice that I had not realized until I experienced greater fluidity and flexibility within my practice. Although this rigidity is in no way inherent to Zen, it existed in my personal interpretation of Zen. I had held monasticism on such a high pedestal that I had attempted to shape myself into something less than the truth of who I am. My efforts to heal the symptoms from the Lyme that had invaded my body made it impossible for me to exist in a false form.

It helped me to move beyond my *ideas* of liberation toward *actual* liberation. I was able to release the faulty story that "only one road leads home." I realized instead that every road leads home if liberation is the goal.

At first, it was difficult for me to control feelings of resentment, resistance, and frustration with my Lyme symptoms. Only later did I understand that I had been given a gift. I needed help to make the shift my heart needed to make. My experience with Lyme invited me to know more of myself and showed me the way. It helped me to open to a spiritual path much greater than I might have otherwise achieved.

Today, when I find myself labeling an unexpected life circumstance or experience as negative, I remind myself of how certain I was once about Lyme. I imagine what my life with Lyme would have been without any stress, worry, resistance, fear, or lack of love. I find my willingness to show up with love to life's challenges even in adverse circumstances.

Every life form needs an advocate. When navigating difficulty, sometimes we can advocate for ourselves and sometimes we have to ask someone with more resources to advocate on our behalf. I was lucky to have a roof over my head and food in my belly every day as I navigated this crisis. When I was the most financially challenged, however, I had no idea how I would afford rent and medicine, and I lost sleep feeling the terror of financial insecurity. Eventually, I sought help from my larger community. I was able to rely on the generosity and creative resourcefulness of a gift economy—an alternative economic model practiced in my community where things were both given as gifts and exchanged in trade. This helped me to get through the hardest times.

Many people today are navigating chronic illness and severe mental, emotional, physical, and spiritual challenges without the support they need to survive. While humanity congratulates itself for having evolved, we have a great deal of work to do in relationship to equity, empathy, community resiliency, and sustainability for disadvantaged people. In today's world, due to the legacy of hierarchy, there are more marginalized people than ever who have been abandoned or let down by the system. Rather than giving our most vulnerable populations, communities, and ecosystems the support they need, we overlook them. At the same time, climate change is creating more economic destabilization and health threats to humanity.

The strength of a thriving ecosystem exists in interdependence, reciprocity, resilience, and the quality of relationships. There is no point in doing the inner work without recognizing ourselves as part of the whole. Personal and collective healing are inextricably linked. Human consciousness can only awaken when we align our way of life with the awareness that we are in this together. It is through slowing down and attuning to our bodies that we access our belonging to and responsibility for the whole.

One of the observations that led to the writing of this book is this: our modern world of shiny lights, computer screens, data, speed, technological progress, and artificial intelligence is only taking us further away from the essential wisdom of our bodies. The good news is that while humans have been distracted by light centricity and speed centricity, *all we need to do to change this focus is slow down and gently shift our attention.* No one owns the rights to the body's natural intelligence. These rights are timeless and shared. This wisdom has remained intact.

* * *

MINDFUL INQUIRY

To what degree do you listen to and honor your body? What signs does your body give you when you need to slow down? What signals does your body give you when you are beginning to feel depleted? What would support you to honor your body's messages more fully?

When has life required you to slow down dramatically at a time that may have felt inconvenient or disappointing? During that time, what was most difficult to let go of? And what hidden gem(s) did you find in the slow and dark once you let go?

What invisible spiritual process—which takes time and cannot be measured or understood—do you find yourself experiencing now? How can you bring more compassion and trust to this slow invisible process?

*   *   *

EXPERIENTIAL PRACTICE: THREE SACRED BREATHS

Pause here for a moment and give yourself permission to take in three of the deepest and slowest breaths that you have taken today. Allow your breath to fill the front of your body, the sides of your body, and the back of your body. Feel your body's connection with gravity. Feel the internal massage of breath moving through your body.

Just by taking a minute to slow down, what did you notice? How do you feel in your body and being? Can you be generous enough with yourself today to pause often, to slow down and take three sacred breaths?

*   *   *

EXPERIENTIAL PRACTICE: THE CENTERS OF YOUR SUBTLE BODY

This is a simple practice of subtle body awareness. I will invite you to bring awareness to or deeply listen to different centers in your body. We will work with the head, throat, heart, belly, and pelvis. Think of these not as parts of your body but as energetic centers. You might associate this with the chakras, and you are welcome to also try this practice with all seven or nine chakras, according to your cosmology. Begin by closing your eyes and turning your attention within. Notice how it feels to rest in darkened stillness. Please take a couple of minutes to settle, paying attention to the breath moving through your body.

Now bring awareness to your head center, starting at the very top of your forehead and sensing into the middle of your forehead. Just listen, sense, and notice. You might be aware of sensation, temperature, color, or shapes. You might notice words, emotions, metaphors, or images. You might have a multi-dimensional technicolor experience. And it's perfectly OK if you notice nothing or numbness. What does numbness actually feel like?

When you feel ready, take in a deep breath, let go of the focus on your head, and then continue to bring awareness to each of your body centers in turn—

your throat, your heart, your belly, and your pelvis—pausing at each to listen, sense, and notice.

How does it feel when you generously and patiently listen to the subtle body with no agenda? How does it feel when you let your body speak to you without interpreting what you hear/sense?

As an alternative, you can do this practice with a partner. One closes their eyes while the other asks them to notice each body center in turn—"What do you notice in your head center?" "What do you notice in your throat center?" and so on—and then simply listens as the person responds. Then you switch roles.

What do you notice?

7

Embracing Change

Creating New Maps through Inner Vision

If you're invested in certainty and security, you are on the wrong path.

PEMA CHÖDRÖN[1]

IN LATE AUTUMN OF 2007, I packed up my few belongings in a duffel bag and boarded a train to traverse the corridor from the monastery in Central California to Los Angeles. Gazing out the window as dawn transformed into day, I watched the gradual transition from farms, prairies, and expansive vistas to the urban bustle and bright lights of the city. Although the monastery was only 350 miles from Los Angeles, the city presented a dramatically different field of consciousness.

Meeting my sister at Union Station downtown, I felt much like I had when traveling around the world at age twenty and taking in the cacophony of sounds, scents, colors, and vibrations of a foreign culture for the very first time. Reorienting to metropolitan Los Angeles after years away, my initial observation was fascination with how palpable the collective thought field was. In contrast to the monastery's silence and stillness, I could literally hear and feel the city buzzing with thought processes.

I would be taking medical leave from the monastery for three months in order to access more sophisticated health care than we had in the countryside. Time to focus on my healing was vital and nonnegotiable. But having lived, breathed, and operated in sacred silence for seven and a half years, I was completely out of my element. Like an anthropologist reimmersing themselves in modern civilization with fresh perception, I witnessed a world ruled by a different set of customs. I observed both the beauty and the suffering in the ways people spoke to each other, interacted and engaged on the streets, related to resources, and carried their bodies in what was considered "the real world" outside the monastic life.

After eight weeks in the city, I had a dream that changed the direction of my life. In this dream I was swimming in a warm body of water that was fairly shallow and nestled against a quiet shoreline. My limbs, starting from the midpoint of my body, began to slowly unfurl and lengthen, extending out like the tentacles of an octopus. As I swam farther out to accommodate my shapeshifting body, I realized then that the body of water I had been swimming in was actually a tiny, protected cove. This cove was isolated from the rest of the sea, which spanned far beyond any point my vision could reach. As the ocean came into greater resolution, I began to see creatures, plants, coral, and myriad forms of life. Sea creatures I had never before encountered began to approach me, seeking connection or needing assistance. The consciousness of the ocean had medicine for me, and I had medicine for the ocean. I realized that this vast ocean was my home and felt the relief of arriving. The cove had become a comfort zone rather than a place of genuine growth. It was time to offer myself in reciprocal engagement with the world, in the spirit of giving back.

I woke up in tears of recognition. Change had pronounced itself. A single thread of clarity had emerged, and I followed. I sensed that my next steps in both service and healing were dependent on leaving the monastery. There was no turning back.

This calling made no sense to my rational mind, which did not understand trading in monastic life to live and teach as a lay person. This calling brought no immediate comfort or gratification, as the "real world" felt terrifying in many ways. This calling made no practical sense, as I had zero income and was navigating a mysterious and sometimes debilitating illness. But my heart had somehow spoken.

A *calling* is a feeling of absolute purpose and inner knowing. It is a vision arising from the pure dark. A calling requires a leap of faith. There is often no measurable or visible evidence that this leap is the right step, yet it speaks to the place within each one of us that feels and senses "rightness" without needing visible evidence. Sometimes a calling affirms the ripeness and *right timing* for a purpose we have long carried or suspected within. Sometimes a calling confidently launches an idea into existence that seems to come from nowhere.

Throughout history, humans have received callings that have required us to step beyond the small self, comfortable identity, and existing plans to act on behalf of something larger yet invisible. I came from a long line of women who had responded to visionary callings that had taken them completely off their set path to be of service. Life had called me to drop everything to devote myself to monasticism. Life was now calling me forth to live and serve in other ways.

A calling beckons our growth toward a particular form, even when we cannot yet see it. We might be pulled into a state of metamorphosis, a phase in which we are unable to recognize where or who we are. Sometimes it requires everything we've got to maintain an invisible thread of trust in the cocoon that leads to our emergence.

Widening Perspective

The dynamic period that followed for me became an intricate dance between trust, doubt, vision, and synchronicity. For the first time after almost eight years of monasticism and twelve years living in earth-based communities outside the conventional monetary economy, I found myself paying rent, navigating doctor's appointments, driving in traffic, socializing, and dealing with the complex bureaucracy of a dispassionate medical system. My intention was *to live in the world without being of the world.* I arose at dawn each day to commune with darkened stillness before the city awoke. I began teaching dharma, sustainable living, and organic gardening and worked part-time for my mother's social justice organization.

As a multidimensional and relational phase of practice began to emerge, I asked myself these questions:

> *What is required to maintain my connection to source in this context?*
> *What is the meeting point between the energetic stillness and deep time of practice and the dynamic chaos of the human world?*
> *How do the teachings of love and no self translate to a context of human existence and relationships in the "real world" and how can these teachings contribute to greater social change?*

This period was one of bold renewal and creation. Through serendipity and word-of-mouth, my work began to spread in ways I could never have imagined. An alternative newspaper published an interview with me, which was followed by an article in the magazine *Yogi Times* and another in the *Los Angeles Times.* Like-minded people began to appear out of nowhere, much like my dream, to collaborate, to volunteer, to offer support, and to cocreate with me. I was still navigating what often felt like excruciating challenges of physical illness and the pressure of living in a world that required money in order to survive, but the resources slowly began to be there as I needed them . . . just enough to help me to trust in my capacity to do what I was made for. I moved into a collective household and found a beautiful community of people sharing resources and values.

In my core, I knew that the monastery was not solely a physical enclosure nestled in the California wilderness. I began to understand that the monastic structure existed within me. I also began to realize the extent to which internal walls had been built in the name of monastic practice. These walls, built of hierarchical perception, were about to be entirely dissolved.

Navigating Change with Grace

Navigating change is a natural part of being human. Everyone who lives long enough has the experience of metaphorically leaving the nest. There comes a moment in everyone's life when things are not what we have come to rely upon or expect. Most people are conditioned to seek security by making the external world as stable as possible, though the degree to which humans can even entertain this idea of security varies dramatically, based on race and class.

While nothing external can actually be relied upon all of the time, the dominant paradigm conditions people to build scaffolding in the form of finding the right job, right home, right relationship, and right amount of money. There is a belief that building scaffolding as quickly as we can creates an external structure that allows us to then relax and be safe.

We try to hold on to these externals. Then, when externals change, we panic. In the face of change, tidal waves of resistance, fear, and conflict can be unleashed in even the most well-intentioned people. Relationships, organizations, and communities often struggle to ride the waves of change.

The alternative is to not invest solely in external security but equally in the only security that is reliable. This is our inner commitment to presence, compassion, and clear seeing . . . our willingness to cultivate a clear heart and clear mind as we navigate life. When we invest in our internal framework by trusting in who we are, we find the strength to endure when the externals change. When we support others to trust in who they are, we support them in finding the strength to endure and adapt to change.

When we invest solely in external scaffolding for security, we diminish our access to a powerful internal framework for navigating change. This internal framework includes fluidity, faith, resiliency, willingness to ask for help, willingness to receive guidance, knowing how to fall, knowing how to fail, and knowing how to let go. This framework is emergent and recognizes that we live in collaboration with life.

The extent to which we suffer as human beings exists in direct correlation to our investment in the *mind of limitation* and *binary perception*. If I had been taught this path directly growing up, my entire journey would have been easier. During the times I thought I was falling or failing, I would have felt less afraid. The moments when I felt directionless, there would not have been accompanying despair. I would have understood that *not knowing* is a valid and safe place to patiently shelter. The times I felt that I was somehow "falling behind," a compassionate mentor would have laughed and pointed out the grand delusion that there is something more valid than my authentic pace or the wisdom of patience.

There is a long-standing belief in the nexus of human consciousness that insists that change, the unknown, and darkness are ultimately to be feared. Historically, personally, and collectively, change has led to loss for many of us. It has also led to positive transformation and renewal—but humanity tends to forget this. In an age where we are collectively called to change old ways, refreshing our framework for navigating change is vital. It is time to collectively let go of our fear of change.

Change can wear the magnificent cloak of a blessing or exhilarating experience such as attaining a new job, discovering an exciting opportunity to pursue a dream we have always held secretly, becoming a parent, or falling in love and merging our life with another. Change can also arrive as an aggressive storm that shatters the security we had believed in. One's partner calls to announce that they are leaving. The results from a medical test arrive announcing terminal illness. A wildfire leaves one's home in burning embers overnight. The ground beneath us that we thought was solid suddenly gets pulled out from under us.

We also live in a world where some people are sheltered much more than others from the sudden loss of security and unwanted change. Some people get hurled into the void brutally and multiple times, in unforeseen ways that shatter their lives. Others have more generous security or support systems built in.

Learning to navigate life's changing nature from center is one of the gifts of endarkenment. Change invites us to affirm our participation with life beyond the isolating, but seemingly sheltered, visible security. With reverence toward the divine darkness, we can learn to meet our human experience of change with openness rather than fear. We can learn to *surrender to* rather than *resist* the groundlessness of change. We can learn to lean into the changing nature of existence, realizing the freedom that arises from *not knowing and realizing we do not have to* fear the unknown.

We can learn to live in a curious, adaptive, and visionary—rather than resistant or fearful—posture. When we choose to stay present through change, we realize that where we are now is the only ground beneath us. We can let go and rest in the now—not knowing, not resisting, not panicking, and not even trying to mentally make sense of things. Beyond our mind's stories, step-by-step, breath by breath, we can trust the now to hold and guide us.

Collectively, there is great opportunity to navigate our changing, complex, seemingly broken world from grace and dignity. We can only do this through a renewed perspective on dark and light. As the forms we have relied upon collectively break down—either personally or globally—there is another option aside from panic. We need not assume fear and resist change. When we look to nature as our teacher, we are reminded that every sustainable ecosystem knows the art of adaptation and collaboration.

The questions to ask yourself are as follows:

When there is no ground beneath me, how can I surrender to groundlessness?
How can I consciously choose not knowing rather than cling to an attempt to know or control?

How can I show up, from center, to the uncertain landscape around me
and take the next step in trust?
What is sturdy, reliable, and steadfast—within me—in the face of every
external change I will experience in this life?
Where, and in what forms, do I need to ask for help or support, as I
navigate change?
How can I meet myself with compassion while I navigate change?

Fearing less as we face change does not mean avoiding our fear of change. We can care for the aspects of our psyche that equate change with loss (think of a scared child or someone who experienced traumatic change in the past), while we simultaneously choose courage. Even with years of monastic training, I sometimes found aspects of my new life frightening.

I affiliated monasticism with everything sacred and holy and feared that living out in the world could dilute my practice. I questioned, at first, my capacity to hold the purity, devotion, and compassionate self-discipline of the Buddha dharma as a lay person. As I navigated health issues, I also sometimes wondered if I would survive in our dispassionate economy.

A mantra I repeated at the time was, *I hold hands with the one who fears change while choosing to courageously take the next step forward in faith. I anchor in the home that is unconditional, the now. I am held by the earth, made whole by my intention, choices, and actions.*

The Principles of Inner Vision

Leaving the monastery was for me a volitional change. It was both uncomfortable and impractical but came from deeper knowing. Because I had no framework or modeling for how to be a monastic living in the world, I had to trust my intuition to guide me. Because there was no road map for my physical healing, I had to recognize the invisible map of emergence. I met this transition one day at a time, embracing the spirit of a pioneer and discoverer. In a sense, this has always been and always remained my practice.

This phase offered a teaching about stepping into the unknown—and being led by the dark. I had no template for this new life but was in touch with the emergent clarity of the map that creates itself in the moment, from darkness and not knowing. *Life creates from the invisible to the visible, rather than the other way around.*

These are useful teachings for navigating personal or collective change. With zero reference for how to be of service amid the challenges we face, divine darkness can offer a map for our collective as we navigate the increasing unknown. There is a critical need for vision, trust, and possibility beyond what humanity has expected and resigned itself to.

There are certain spiritual principles through which we are led by divine darkness. Before sharing these encouragements, I acknowledge that these principles have arisen through my own practice and life experience. And even when I've navigated the most difficult, seemingly brutal heartbreaking transitions of my life, I've continually had the systemic support of white privilege. Therefore, depending on your own personal history, background, and life circumstances, please harvest what feels useful and essential from these teachings, while acknowledging that my context for change is limited to my life experience.

The following are spiritual principles through which we are led by divine darkness:

- **Most importantly, we have to be willing to be vulnerable in the face of change.** Groundlessness is the seat of both vulnerability and absolute possibility.
- **We have to let go of story and rest in not knowing**. The surface narrative—of fear, doubt, or what-if—maintains our insistence on limiting beliefs. Feeding the stories in our head upholds our obedience to the loud authority of the conditioned mind. Resting in "I don't know" can feel uncomfortable at first, yet it positions us

to listen more deeply within. This is how we begin to reclaim our internal authority.

- **We must declare our heart's intention, without being attached to outcome.** In other words, the place to invest our energy and faith is intention. Intention gives our life force an essential focus. It does not serve, however, to be attached to how the product of our intention looks. The attitude to cultivate is *I will be OK if this manifests. I will be OK if it does not.* I offer my heart's intention to the invisible realm and allow life to show me the visible path and form this might take. This is symbolized by a soft open hand, both willing to receive and willing to let go.

- **Life is an emergent process.** This may seem obvious, but many of us are conditioned to focus on reaching a destination or conclusion as quickly as possible, often bypassing vital steps along the way. We can instead learn to trust our emergent experience as it unfolds. We can savor the process of receiving guidance in the moment and then again in the next moment.

- **While ego seeks immediate gratification and visible external evidence that we are OK or going in the right direction, there is another way.** We can trust the invisible confirmation that arises through intuition, guidance, and insight. We can trust our felt sense of moving in our true direction. This requires paying attention to subtle body awareness.

- **"Thy will, not my will."** Life's directive does not always feel comfortable to us or make sense to us at the time. It does not always tell us what we wish to hear. Sometimes it tells us exactly the opposite. Yet our willingness to discern between life's will rather than ego's will can strengthen our sense of trust in who we really are. It fortifies our commitment to act on behalf of consciousness, as part of something larger than our small/separate self.

- **Direct revelation or inner vision requires conscious boundaries.** We have to be willing to stop seeking information from the imagined expert "out there." This can take the form of someone else's advice. It can be the religious code of right versus wrong. It can be a disrupting voice of doubt. It can be the distracting screen that keeps us from listening more deeply within for our own conviction.

- **We may need to let go, again and again, of our ideas about timing in order to honor nature's timing.** Releasing the linear progression that we are hoping for can make space for life's natural progression to emerge.
- **We must stay in touch with wonder, curiosity, and fascination.** We can ask life to support us and be continually surprised by the forms support takes and the sources from which it arrives.
- **Cultivating partnership with nature dissolves the illusion of separation and isolation.** Partnership with nature equates to reciprocal cocreation with life. This begins with asking for support—not for our ego's purpose but for our deeper purpose. If we are willing, we can invite and receive support from not only our human community but our ancestors and future beings, from not only allies we recognize visibly but also the invisible and subconscious realms and from the medicinal world of plants, minerals, fungi, insects, animals, and beyond, discounting none of the nexus of nature's intelligence.

This guidance serves not only when we face uncertainty and change. It serves through every life experience we want to meet from presence and possibility. To start from the basis of not knowing is honest. Only when we are comfortable enough in emptiness or groundlessness can we let go of the "need to solve, know, fix, conclude, or assert our will"—often meaningless efforts that prevent access to life's guidance. To receive guidance, we must make space for the empty, dark, and formless—the unknown.

We often focus on achieving the end goal to avoid discomfort. But this discomfort is where possibility lives. It feels too vulnerable to recognize that life is always an unfinished, formless process. When our focus is on the finished product, however, we risk missing out on life in the moment.

Likewise, when we are listening to or witnessing someone in the midst of difficulty, we can find ourselves wanting to help solve their problems as quickly as possible. Because perceived problems make us feel uncomfortable, we often immediately offer advice or solutions instead of *being fully present* with their process. We forget that presence and deep listening are the most generous expressions of love we can offer anyone. We strive to resolve conflict as efficiently as possible, sometimes avoiding the multidimensionality and emotionality of it as a result.

The world was forever changed by the COVID-19 pandemic. As the introduction of vaccines led to a new phase in the pandemic, however, people wanted to return to "business as usual" as quickly as possible, although there was still no solid ground. It made the human psyche feel too vulnerable to remain in a state of formless inconclusive change. There was no actual return to life as it had been, however, because there were new and continually changing components to navigate.

Endarkenment reveres the mystery as the seat of life's intelligence rather than a burden to bear and fear. It's okay to experience life's unfinished, unresolved, and unfolding process. To rest in the dark often, without trying to reach the light, is wisdom. Only when we are willing to remain in the dark do we realize that we're okay there. It is by experiencing vulnerability that we remember the maternal embrace of interdependence.

Life's intelligence arises from darkness. Possibility, healing, and fresh insight form in the dark. New formations and new connections are made in the dark, beyond anything our ego could imagine.

There are so many ways that we try to avoid the vulnerability of that which is unformed. Although we all seek to be coparticipants in this divine orchestra of life, we have been conditioned to believe that it is weak to cease control and let life show us the way. Perhaps the greatest joy of being human, however, is our lived experience of participation and moment-to-moment cocreation and sharing in life. Here are a few suggestions for doing so:

- When immersed in a creative project, patiently bring that project into the restful state of incubation. Do not dishonor creative energy with undue force or excessive mental assessment.
- When in conversation with one another, allow yourselves to rest in the spaciousness from which connection arises. Beyond the assumption that words are better than silence, beyond any pressure to connect, beyond fear of awkwardness, trust the empty space of intimacy without trying to fill this space.
- When making love, slow down radically and let go of the script. It is the meeting point between spaciousness and erotic curiosity that allows every move, touch, and expression to be electric and healing.
- In meditation, do not exert unnecessary effort to try to attain the light. This, too, is a way of filling space. The light was never lost, so it cannot be found.

Dark Nights and the Thinning of the Veil

For a seed to achieve its greatest expression it must come completely undone. The shell cracks, its insides come out, and everything changes. To someone who doesn't understand growth it would look like pure destruction.

CYNTHIA OCCELLI[2]

Spiritual traditions across the world recognize "dark times," periods that appear as the absence of light, yet also offer a profound invitation for growth. In times of perceived darkness, our familiar comfort and sense of security become disrupted, and we find ourselves navigating the unknown. While it can feel like there is nothing to hold on to while swimming through the mysterious tides of life transition, loss, or illness, there is always a choice. It is because we have nothing familiar to hold on to that we can open our hearts to fresh and nonhabitual forms of perception. These moments can become the most potent opportunities for insight, healing, and transformation that we might ever experience.

The phrase "dark night of the soul" describes a spiritual crisis in one's journey toward God. While this crisis is usually temporary, it can endure for a long period of time. We might enter a dark night of the soul—a period that feels particularly absent/void of light, clarity, and well-being—after experiencing a loss, in the depression after a painful breakup, or in a significant life transition. Although it may take strength we feel we do not have, we can realize the spiritual opportunity of a dark night as a passageway for unforeseen growth and renewal. A dark night often invokes the shedding of familiar skin or identity. By both surrendering to and seeking support for the dark night we are enveloped in, we can awaken to the gift of endarkenment that I have shared through these writings.

The path of European shamanism that I practice teaches *dismemberment*. This is a ritual that takes place regularly through a shamanic journey. In this journey, in the invisible, imaginal realm, one consciously invites a spiritual ally to completely decimate one's physical form. One surrenders to their physical form dissolving, as an experience of conscious death. The formlessness and groundlessness that follow puts one in touch with the vast, boundless, and unlimited nature of being. Free of form, one experiences a deep renewal and returns again to physical form.

Dismemberment is related to *rites of passage*, a term first coined by the Dutch-German-French anthropologist Arnold van Gennep. Rites of passage are "dying practices" we can engage in while living—in preparation for the physical death that awaits all of us at the end of our lives. We experience rites of passage, intentionally or unintentionally, through those experiences that metaphorically present death, the liminal states in between, and a rebirth. Sometimes we experience rites of passages and dismemberments intentionally, and sometimes unintentionally, through loss, illness, dramatic spiritual awakenings, or the winds of change.

As we explored, humans tend to dislike being neither here nor there. When we leave the familiar shore without the far shore yet in view, we are left with the discomfort of *liminality*. *Limen*, the Latin root of the word *liminality*, means "threshold."[3] It is the threshold that separates one space from another. It is the space between that we sometimes try to fill in meditation and practice, because that space makes us uncomfortable. The word *liminality* is used to describe the process of transitioning psychologically and spiritually across borders and boundaries. The liminal states between can serve as unique opportunities to access the strength of our inner light. Through liminality, change happens.

This connects to the Buddhist concept of the bardos. The word *bardo* refers to both the liminal states we enter after death before rebirth and those times when our usual way of life becomes suspended as, for example, during a period of illness or grief or during a meditation retreat or awakening. External constraints and life as we know it dissolve, and we find ourselves in unexpected transition. As our ego's hold on reality becomes challenged, we can experience a significant shift in perspective and perception.

In the bardos, we can experience the activation of and support offered to a human life, an animated human body, through comfort from what is beyond the known.

Because we will die one day—and because life is constant change—it is helpful to learn to consciously engage in bardo experiences. Buddhist practice recognizes the bardo as a valuable training and place of transmission. Through this process, we can become familiar with the liminality that is essential to living and dying.

In the words of Suzuki Roshi,

When you bow, bow
Sit, sit
When on a dark night, surrender to the journey of the soul
Take the fetal position.[4]

Partnership with Nature

When we look to the natural world as our teacher, we see that to be adaptive is to sustain life.

Every ecosystem and life form that models sustainability and resiliency operates in collaboration. Honeybees, dandelions and butterflies, and mushrooms and their mycelial network model intricately intelligent systems of collaboration. For instance, the honeybee exists as part of the organism of the hive, even when pollinating a flower ten miles away. Similarly, birds don't map out their flights or migrations, they experience a feeling in their body, and this guides them to operate wisely and in unison with their flock.

Consider metaphorically that it is when we give our attention to, or become distracted by, the conditioned mind that we lose the home base of hive intelligence. Human conditioning has promoted a sense of isolation and separation in competition with others for survival, while following a predetermined and linear template. This could not be further from the truth.

The invitation of spiritual practice today is to live in presence and partnership with nature. Partnership with nature means engaging in a reciprocal conversation with life in order to serve life. Just as it takes a village to raise a child, I believe it takes a community to remember who we are. In the words of the biologist Janine Benyus, "If we are to use our tools in the service of fitting in on Earth, our basic relationship to nature—even the story we tell ourselves about who we are in the universe—has to change."[5]

Partnership with nature requires that we are first anchored in the moment. From presence, we access beginner's mind and the wonder required to converse respectfully with other forms of life and consciousness. It is not as simple as asking for support and receiving it. It's about the sincerity and humility with which we seek support. It's about the quality of the questions we ask and the quality with which we listen and receive guidance.

From presence, we know ourselves to be instruments for benevolent friendship and collaboration with life. We know the love we embody can be touched by and extend to all forms of life.

One of my teachers used to say, "If you want to find water, it is better to stand in one place and dig deep, rather than digging a bunch of shallow wells." This encouragement is instructive in an age when spiritual materialism and "chasing experience" are popular. There can be a tendency to seek out exotic experiences through spirituality rather than digging deep. Once you have a deep practice, you also have a foundation from which to invite other forms into your medicine chest, if you choose to.

When I contracted Lyme, I had already given my life to living in presence. I knew how to work in partnership with nature through, for example, listening deeply to the organic gardens I stewarded and my commitment to sustainable living. I imposed, however, an unnecessary rigidity onto Zen practice. I sometimes put acceptance on a pedestal over possibility and the creative imagination, thus limiting the full expression of partnership with nature I was to grow into. Through hierarchical perception I sometimes discounted guidance received from my body and the invisible realm in favor of the monastery's guidance or a Buddhist text.

In order to heal, I had to fully let go of the lines I drew around monasticism and generously expand my circle of support. This meant being willing to ask for support from every form of life imaginable. I was required to commit to my current relationships, as well as form new relationships, with allies in both the visible and invisible realms. Healing support appeared in the form of plants, animals, insects, minerals, ancestors, spirit allies, and the elements. My willingness to expand my fluency in the language of the wild, the subconscious, and the domain of nocturnal dreams allowed for my healing to bear fruit.

One of the most important turning points in my healing process was a dream in which I found myself in an expansive desert landscape of cacti and sagebrush. I was walking toward a small earthen shelter, much like the rammed earth shelters at the monastery. I opened the handmade wooden door to find the space completely empty inside except for a simple altar in front of a single window. This window opened not to the light of day outside but to the ancient spirit of darkness herself. I gazed into the infinite darkness with a sense of gazing backward into time. I had the feeling of waiting for someone to arrive, and I felt joyful anticipation.

From the darkness emerged a female figure, who identified herself as a distant ancestor from my mother's mother's lineage of Eastern European descent. This ancestor was a farmer, whose physical somatic connection with the earth was so fiercely intact it transmitted to me something that I had always longed for. She was the embodiment of the deep feminine entirely free of conditioning. She modeled the absolute vitality that comes from the primal experience of human embodiment, beyond the ego.

This ancestor placed seeds in the palm of my hand and proceeded to show me that I was made for seed planting. She said, "While your dharma teacher's teachers held the task of protecting the seeds of dharma and lineage, your task and the task of your generation is different. Your task is to plant seeds in the world to evolve change and healing. Like permaculture, your generation needs to sow dharma seeds in ways that might one day transform the institutions and paradigm of your world. These seeds come to you through visions, dreams, and your creative imagination. In the name of personal and collective healing, you have to be willing to bring them forward and to cross-pollinate across lines you have created in your own mind." This ancestor has been with me since, and her message continues to inform my life's work.

The Democracy of Darkness Leaves No Part Out

Watching the moon at midnight,
solitary, mid-sky,
I knew myself completely
No part left out.
IZUMI SHIKIBU[6]

The democracy of darkness includes everything. It is the radical field of nondiscrimination that leaves nothing and no one out.

Part of my purpose in writing this book is to acknowledge the importance of *leaving no part out*—in spiritual practice or in life. The meeting point between ancient teachings and modernity has left a landscape of confusing edges within contemporary spirituality. For instance, not only has Western appropriation of Buddhism/dharma led to mistranslation and misunderstanding of original practices but in addition, most historical Buddhist texts were written by male monastics. Historically, monastic life was considered the purest, most concentrated form of practice. In early Buddhism, women were not even considered able to be enlightened. The *Mahayana sutra*, specifically the fourth-century Bodhisattvabhumi, states that "a woman who is about to attain enlightenment will be reborn as a male."[7] Although Western spiritual practice has long been dominated by white male leadership, today people of all genders practice Buddhist and secular dharma, the majority as lay practitioners. Within Buddhism, even today, however, lay practice is considered secondary, with lay teachers not even ordained in certain lineages.

As we have explored throughout this book, because of the intersubjective nature of conditioning, we often do not see the unconscious biases that exist within our minds and our communities. We all carry internalized biases and residue from the imbalance of patriarchy and other manifestations of hierarchical perception. The author and social activist bell hooks defines patriarchy as "a political-social system that insists that males are inherently dominating."[8] Because patriarchy has for so long dictated how things are done and what template is followed, we might hold subtle internal biases we are not even aware of that keep us from knowing the regenerative balance of the sacred masculine and feminine within. In other words, regardless of gender, the balance and strengths of the elemental masculine or feminine are not available to us if we hold one way of being as higher than the other. We might experience patriarchal conditioning as a constriction or pressure, a sense of standards we should meet, or we might experience it through judgment toward others. This imprint exists in each of our psyches to some degree, in our spiritual and secular communities, and in the cultures humans have created.

I suggest you pause here and notice how the term *patriarchy* impacts you. It can be enriching and liberating to investigate the subtle ways each of us might have internalized any biases that come from patriarchal perception. It is equally insightful to pay attention to the complexity of emotions this term can evoke including anger, criticism, defensiveness, or other emotions. Because the term sometimes gets used in a dualistic or judgmental way, people can misinterpret it as antimasculine. The naming of patriarchy is not antimasculine but rather anti–male dominance and pro-equity. The purpose of investigating hierarchical perception is always to bring us back into balance and wholeness that is our birthright, not to make one half of our nature wrong.

Within Buddhism and in our world today, we are just beginning to recognize many communities that have been previously excluded or discounted, and who need greater inclusivity. In addition to women, these include the BIPOC and LGBTQIA+ communities, disabled people, low-income and disadvantaged communities, and other ethnic minorities. In Zen Buddhism practice, for example, recognition is needed in response to unique life experiences, challenges, and/or cultural heritage. People of diverse backgrounds might benefit from more relatable translations of the teachings, in voices they recognize as their own, and that acknowledge the specific path, trauma, and injustices their families and ancestors might have endured. While this might not be the experience of all BIPOC peoples, I have come to understand that this is true for some, possibly most, especially in the United States.

On a personal level, spiritual practice can reveal ways we have internalized the exclusivity of patriarchy. For example, we might mistranslate the essence of a teaching through a conditioned filter of right versus wrong rather than nonduality. Rather than bringing our unique self fully to *sangha*, we might try to fit the shape of what we see modeled and hold it as the standard.

We might elevate a teacher or monk to such a high pedestal that we sacrifice our own needs or inner knowing. In so doing, we pay respect externally, while disrespecting ourselves internally. There is a fine line between holding a person or institution with honor, respect, and devotion and upholding unconscious hierarchical perception. To learn how to humbly receive guidance is vital to establishing a spiritual practice; however, when we put anyone on a pedestal, including ourselves, we no longer see clearly.

Discipleship is a sacred tradition, yet, due to the legacy of *power over*, awareness must be brought to teacher-student and community relationships. Sometimes people collude with abuse of power in an organization out of misplaced devotion. Sometimes people shy away from questioning the integrity of a teacher or institution upon witnessing questionable actions, for fear of rejection. The alternative is to commit to transparency, reciprocity, right use of power, and accountability in every spiritual organization. There needs to be transparency about the complexity and paradoxes of a person or institution we hold dear. When we project undefiled, untouchable perfection onto our teachers, mentors, and leaders, however, we miss the opportunity to know them as whole humans, who can teach us both through their strengths and their vulnerabilities.

In my own experience with this faulty hierarchical perception, I held the teachings and institution of Zen Buddhism on such a high pedestal that I was afraid to bring every part of me in. As I delved even deeper, I found myself afraid to question aspects of the culture created around the practice that did not always resonate with the essence of practice.

It was my experience with Lyme disease that set me on a spiritual pilgrimage to instigate the integration of my whole self. It was the unexpected bite of a tick that encouraged me to turn toward those parts of me that I had failed to recognize. Sometimes we remain completely ignorant of aspects of ourselves that we might not have realized exist until we receive the first sign of reconnection. We might become aware of a quiet yearning—the sense of a seed of possibility within that feels, at the same time, like a distant memory. Until that part is brought into our awareness—into complete inclusion within our psyche—we may not realize we had been starving for a wholeness we were missing.

Western shamanism recognizes *soul loss* as the contraction, abandonment, or exclusion of aspects of our being that can occur through life's traumas. For instance, if as a child, in a moment of pure freedom and excitement, we were harshly told to be still, we might experience *soul loss*. We learn to fear and mistrust freedom.

Soul retrieval, in Western shamanism, is the ritual practice for retrieving lost parts, when they are ready to return. Meditation gives us a similar experience of soul retrieval by continuously meeting lost parts of ourselves with *compassion*, thus inviting them back in. We remember that what we are made of in the first place is the consciousness of darkness or inclusivity.

Even more meaningful than the experience of retrieving a missing part is the continual process itself of becoming the force of reclamation. It is life-changing to reclaim a lost part of us, but we do not need to stop there. Or think that we have arrived. Or cling to it. We begin to realize, over time, that who we are is as vast as the entire universe—a universe that is ours to reclaim.

My reclamation began with a reorientation to dharma that celebrated the potential of embodiment. This meant turning to my subtle body as ultimate authority and being willing to listen without wavering. It meant realizing that my body had more shared power and relational intelligence stored within it than I had ever imagined. It meant no longer allowing the fantasy of authority to deter me from the authority of my heart. And it meant no longer being afraid of the power I embodied.

My reclamation included relationships, friendships, and a celebration of community as the path itself. It included honoring the expressive and relational aspects of my nature equally to the still and contemplative. It included a wholehearted embrace of sexuality, sensuality, and erotic intelligence with a renewed understanding of the importance of these domains to my personal and collective healing. Taking refuge in eros was an expression of placing Gaia herself at the center of my temple. My reclamation included spiritual partnership and eventually marriage as part of my dharma path. It also included holding equally the earth-based, animistic, and shamanic practices which had for a long time occupied a quieter place in my life. I had held the practice of Zen on an exclusive pedestal that served only to maintain the delusion of hierarchical perception.

My reclamation included the *deep feminine*. By "deep feminine" I do not mean the culturally implied gender-based qualities, archetypes, or expectations. I am talking about the elemental feminine—the embodiment of the restorative, regenerative, receptive wisdom of the body and relational forms of knowing. Living in a cultural tradition that had been male dominated for twenty-six hundred years, it is no surprise that I had overlooked and excluded the deep feminine. And only by restoring the deep feminine within myself was I able to equally reclaim the *elemental* or *sacred masculine*, thus embodying a balance that has brought immeasurable joy to my life.

Over the subsequent years, bringing my whole self in brought me more joy than I could ever have imagined and informed my work as a dharma teacher. It transpired into teaching and guiding others in relational mindfulness and authoring two books. It gave birth to a body of practice that has transformed the lives of many individuals, couples, families, sanghas, and organizations. I committed, as a dharma teacher, to generously guiding retreats about sacred sexuality and erotic intelligence, as this was so often excluded in my own practice. I devoted myself to guiding the Work That Reconnects, as a response the social-ecological crisis we face. I committed to teaching deep feminine-centered, regenerative leadership and to guiding a sangha devoted to both presence and partnership with nature, celebrating the wisdom of Zen in collaboration with earth-based practices.

*　*　*

MINDFUL INQUIRY

When have you experienced a major life transition as a sacred rite of passage? Please hold this time in your awareness and reflect on it. What were you required to let go of through that transition? What emerged through that transition? What inner qualities and strengths supported you in navigating this rite of passage?

Think of a change you are facing today. What arises within you or gets triggered in the face of this change? What stories, body sensations, and feelings? Please take in three deep breaths and consider the following: How can you support yourself to stay present through this transition? What part(s) of you most needs compassion and reassurance as you navigate this change? What might you be required to let go of in order to accept this change?

Now consider what gets triggered within you in the face of global uncertainty. What stories, body sensations, and emotions arise? Please take in three deep breaths, feeling and noticing what arises within you. Gently turn toward and feel compassion for the part of you that is struggling. Consider how you can support yourself to stay present as we face global uncertainty. What would support you to stay grounded and well-resourced? How might you ask for support from the people in your life? From the natural world? From your own true nature?

* * *

EXPERIENTIAL PRACTICE: FINDING REFUGE
IN THE WOMB OF THE NATURAL WORLD

This practice requires at least one hour of your time, as well as a journal and blindfold. If you are a person with a disability, wheelchair user, or someone who is homebound, you are welcome to engage in this practice through visualization. You can give yourself the same experience through your imagination without physically traveling.

Pick a place in nature that is dark and feels safe. You might pick a grove of shady trees, a cave, or a hammock beneath the night sky. Give yourself some time to connect with your breath, body, and darkened stillness. Begin to open your awareness to the qualities of this dark place. Notice the restorative qualities of nature surrounding you. Notice how it feels in your body to rest here. Give yourself permission to relax even more deeply. Take all the time you need *to receive the restoration of this dark place. If you would like to, you can put on a blindfold and rest here for a period of time in even more concentrated darkness.*

Ask yourself, If this place had words, what would it be expressing to me? *It might be as simple as* You are beloved. You are not alone. You are a precious part of the whole.

Take as much time as you would like. When you are ready, take in a few deep breaths to transition. Offer thanks to this place. Write down any reflections or insights that arose from this practice.

PART FOUR

Restoring Wholeness in Ourselves and Our World

COLLECTIVE ENDARKENMENT

*The challenges we face—climate change, species extinc-
tion, and a legacy of systemic racism, to name a few—
are not ones we can meet solely through the mind of
logic and rationalization. These challenges cannot be
navigated alone but are calling us out of isolation into
relational forms of knowing. The chapters in this part
explore darkness as a source of wisdom for our collective
in changing times and speak of human relationship,
leadership, moral imagination, and the imperative to
befriend and let go of fear in order to embrace emergence.*

8

Relational Intelligence

Seeing Each Other Clearly in the Dark

flowers are silent. silence is silent. the mind is a silent flower.
the silent flower of the world opens.

IKKYU SOJUN[1]

FOR MANY YEARS, I led retreats in the hidden hills of Matilija Canyon, in Ojai, California. Arriving at this secluded refuge, after a long, winding drive up historical Route 33, felt like landing on another planet. There was nothing around for miles except a small Zen center at the very end of a dirt road.

The quality of silence in this chaparral riparian landscape of low-growing sage, yucca, and cactus felt otherworldly. The canyon seemed to emphasize the endless sky more than the land below.

On the opening night of a silent retreat, as the sun set over the Topa-Topa Mountains, I invited participants to sit in a circle in the meditation hall. The room was lit only by candles. As dusk descended into darkness, we meditated together, allowing our bodies and minds to synchronize.

The room was filled with anticipation for the inner journey we were about to embark on. For many participants, it felt like coming home, as they had practiced in this sacred place with me for years.

After a period of time, I invited the group to pass a ceremonial stone from the canyon around the circle, each taking the time they needed to listen within and share their heart's intention for our journey together over the coming days. The group experienced one another's presence without visually seeing one another. In the disarming darkness, people could fully witness and be witnessed by each other.

The darkness provided a canvas to notice and savor the unique quality of each person's presence. Beyond surface perception, we listened to the pace, tone, energy, and emotions expressed through someone's voice— the vulnerability and courage in their words and the quality with which they listened to themselves as they spoke. The darkness offered relief from social habits and expectations that can feed self-consciousness and distance people from one another. Free of the cloak of separation, we felt our shared unified presence.

People often monitor and judge themselves and others on appearance or surface qualities when socializing. It is typical for humans to try to impress or outdo one another with academic titles, certificates, a special identity, pronouncements of what seem to them to be "wise words," or a recitation of accomplishments in their lives. This habit of trying to be seen at our best and avoid being seen at our worst creates a protective shield against genuine connection. If we are preoccupied by assessment of self or other, we cannot settle into genuine connection. We cannot enjoy just being human together. Every relationship we will ever have begins with the quality of our relationship with ourselves. *Intimacy within allows us to be intimate with one another and with our world.*

Practice invites us to *show up* just as we are, in each moment, rather than trying to look good, sound wise, or impress. During retreat, we pause from socializing, from expressing our opinions or trying to get attention from others. We practice *custody of the eyes*, letting go of the tendency to watch other people or wonder if we are being watched. With our attention turned within, we can bring awareness to the unnecessary preoccupation with the self and the suffering caused by these habits so we can let them go. While social connection offers its own meaningful reward, experiencing silent community offers a depth of connection that humans crave—connection without effort or activity. We rest in the stillness that is the seat of life's intimacy. Metaphorically in the dark, we can engage with one another's felt energetic presence rather than one another's personality.

Going beyond Hierarchical Perception

Darkness is the invisible field of unity beyond discrimination. Relational intelligence and authentic leadership grow in the dark. Darkness, physically or metaphorically, invokes a vulnerability that connects us to our shared human experience. In darkness, we are freer from social programming. We don't have to present a smile or perfect complexion or image of self-confidence. We don't have to present an overlay of any image on our ordinary self or essence. Instead, we can show up as we are and rest in the poetry and mystery of life together.

When I teach leadership, I invite people to release the idea of presenting—either themselves or a speech. Instead, I teach people to show up as they are, listen and speak from the heart, and be guided by the moment. This could be likened to the experience of "showing up naked." Instead of preparing an offering (featuring the perfect presentation/program or highlighting our intelligence or accomplishments), we can show up empty. We offer ourselves as a vessel for consciousness to lead *through* us, in an emergent way. In my experience, showing up naked as a leader has meant showing up exactly as I am, without a mask on, without hiding in the esteemed role of leader in any way. It has meant showing up without making it about me but instead surrendering myself to the shared field of energy of the group I am guiding. I might have an intention for what I am teaching and even a structure/outline for what I am presenting, but the emphasis is on speaking from the heart and staying present to the moment-by-moment emergent group experience.

In the relational field, our sense of separation occurs when we begin to label, judge, categorize, and compare. The very moment we step into the field of judgment or comparison, we leave the present, the now. Perhaps we label something we admire in someone else; we then compare ourselves to this quality and come up short. Perhaps we identify something in another person that we don't like; we then perceive ourselves as superior.

Whatever conclusion we come to is a delusion. We have left *whole-mind perception* to instead feed *the mind of separation*. We have settled on a conclusion or idea based on binary perception. We trade in the poetry of the full spectrum each person embodies for a binary label—special or not special, good or bad, light or dark.

Generally, the conclusions we come to support and repeat whatever our habitual karmic tendency is at that moment in our lives. In other words, if we are someone who feels inadequate, this will be projected onto the relational field. If we are someone who believes they are misunderstood, part of our psyche will scan the relational field for proof of this belief. If we have an arrogance or superiority complex, this too will be projected onto the relational field.

Whole mind perceives wholeness. Any self-evaluation involving judgment about what is beloved and desirable and what is unloved or undesirable is delusional. As in meditation, likes and dislikes can still exist, but we experience life as a unified field, rather than pitting diverse qualities against each other.

Beyond Every Label Is Nonseparation

Behind and beyond every label is empty space. Spacious awareness is the connective tissue that binds together all of life. The living tapestry of interconnection is the backdrop of every moment. It can take time to find this space, but it is always here. It is our natural state. We experience it as feeling connected to source rather than tangled in the mind's overlays and subjective interpretations.

Source is the place from which everything originates. Think of it as consciousness itself. To be connected to source is the felt experience of being present, conscious, and connected with what we might call nature's pulse or life force moving through us. We also might experience this as a sense of the divine. It is the experience of consciousness knowing itself. From source connection, our experience can contain myriad layers and concurrent experiences, but it is all held in wholeness. Being connected to source is a very ordinary human experience, but it can also have mystical dimensions.

There are not enough accurate words in the English language to describe this state, although it is often referred to as nonduality. We access it through direct experience. We find it not through thinking but by attending to the space between our thoughts. We realize it in knowing ourselves as consciousness itself, the vessel through which our experience traverses.

We might experience nonduality when gazing at the sky, equally aware of the individual clouds moving through it, the backdrop of the sky itself, and the ever-changing nature of movement—and we can't help but realize that we too are part of the sky. Or we might experience it when standing in a forest, simultaneously aware of a tree, the entire forest, the oxygen from the trees entering our own lungs, and the realization that we are one shared coemergent field. We also remember nonduality in a moment of pure intimacy with a loved one, when the sense of me versus you drops away and the shared body of presence emerges instead. And we remember it when we shift from binary perception to being the witness, moving from this *versus* that, to this *and* that.

Full-Spectrum Living: There Is Dark in the Light and Light in the Dark

Life is a continuous spectrum of light and dark. From the gradation of night and day to every destination in between, life is a continuum. From the dark night to the daylight of the soul, these are continuums. From the restoration of stillness to the expressiveness of action, humans exist on a spectrum.

In the words of Thomas Moore in *Dark Nights of the Soul*, "Every human life is made up of the light and the dark, the happy and the sad, the vital and the deadening. How you think about this rhythm of moods makes all the difference."[2]

Life presents myriad experiences day and night where light and dark are overlapping and interwoven. We might be aware of the fleeting nature of life at the same time that we feel elation. I often experience tears of joy in the presence of my five-year-old nephew, whose light is so radiant and exuberant that it blasts my heart open. I experience the beauty and luminosity of the winter's sky in a unique way, touched deep within by the soft subtle light amid a more barren landscape.

The ancient symbol for the Tao beautifully illustrates the whole of the yin and yang curled around each other, with each element containing an eye of the other at its very center. It also captures the complete absence of polarization and duality in life.

Consider human consciousness. We have myriad emotions, some of which are lighter and some of which are darker. In the center of the light experience of joy, there exists a dark spot of impermanence.

In the words of the author Richard Paul Evans, "Sunsets, like childhood, are viewed with wonder not just because they are beautiful but because they are fleeting."[3] Remember the happiness of childhood on the last day of summer? Perhaps you can recall feeling happy while being aware simultaneously that tomorrow you returned to school.

The Tao exists in every experience of lovemaking and sacred sexuality. The pleasure of *eros* literally arises from the dark. Within the ecstasy existing between two well-tuned lovers, there can be recognition that this chemistry is rare. Or that while we were made for this degree of concentrated aliveness, we may not be experiencing it in every waking moment. The light of ecstasy coexists with the recognition of a primordial power so full that perhaps it remains hidden some of the time.

Humor, too, is a marriage between light and dark, comedy and trag-edy. There is no humor—from foolish slapstick to dry, cerebral jokes that delight the mind—that is not based on the understanding that all things must pass. In every humorous exchange or thought, there is a delicate arrow pointing to mortality. Even watching a clown slip on a banana peel in slapstick comedy evokes a metaphor for death, the fall, or the loss of our equilibrium.

At the very center of laughter's medicine, there exists a spot of dark-ness. That darkness is the emptiness or hunger within each of us, longing for the brilliant or outrageous nourishment of laughter. Similarly, when we engage in play, we feel a giddy lightness that comes from our engage-ment with the *imaginal realm*, yet we also experience a spot of darkness in the middle. Sometimes we laugh so hard, we cry.

Recognizing that all of life is a spectrum allows us to accept and celebrate fully our human experience. Life is short, so our willingness to embrace everything in our experience is vitally important. When we let go of *binary perception,* we can honor the multidimensionality, depth, and poetry of who we actually are. Immeasurable joy and gratitude can exist simultaneously with grief for the suffering in our world. The entire time I was experiencing the debilitating impact of Lyme disease on my body, I simultaneously expe-rienced tremendous joy, gratitude, love, and vibrant aliveness. Difficult life circumstances can coexist alongside grace, trust, and hope.

When new meditators begin to integrate stillness into their everyday lives, they often discover how much room there actually is inside of them. In stillness, they find that there is space for their feelings to exist. There is room for other people's reactions to exist and for the demands of life to exist. In stillness, they don't have to do something about everything but instead can invite it all into spaciousness—and do so with compassion. This stillness turns out to be a much more powerful place than they had realized. It can hold the full and limitless spectrum.

Full-spectrum living means to embrace our whole selves and to under-stand that in being human we contain it all. The Buddha taught that each one of us contains everything that has happened to all of humanity since before the beginning of beginningless time. This includes a tremendous amount of love and joy . . . and unfathomable suffering.

This remembrance allows us to meet one another from a much freer place. We can show up as we are, without judging ourselves and one another as either light or dark, strong or weak, good or bad. We do not have to judge others or hide ourselves to keep them from judging us. We can let go of the energy-draining and self-absorbed activity of continuous self-improvement. Instead, we can learn to relax, without having to constantly monitor how we present to others.

When I first left the monastery, it felt odd to me that people would often ask, "How are you?" I found myself feeling pressured to categorize how I felt in response, to label my experience at the moment. At the monastery, when the question "How are you?" was asked, it meant "In this moment, deep down, how is your body-mind-heart?" Out in the world again, I gave myself permission to answer truthfully but simply: "I'm feeling a lot of gratitude, and I'm also feeling tender about our world today. I'm really enjoying my creative process, and I'm also feeling an uncomfortable surge of self-doubt."

Not only did this break up the tendency toward small talk, but it invited others to pause, look within, and respond from a more honest place as well.

Waking Up from Hierarchical Perception

Many paths lead from the foot of the mountain, but at
the peak we all gaze at the single bright moon.
IKKYU SOJUN[4]

We have all been traumatized to varying degrees by the *lens of hierarchy*. This lens asserts high and specific standards that are completely relative and artificial—maintained by an invisible contract that requires our participation. This lens presents superiority versus inferiority in the form of race, class and income, gender, sexual orientation, religion, profession, age, and appearance. Superiority versus inferiority is judged through one's level of education, degree of extroversion versus introversion, physical/mental/emotional ability, size and body type, marital or relationship status, number of credentials or certificates, level of closeness to people in authority or who are rich or famous, and the list goes on.

One's place in this hierarchy is determined by what degree one fits into hegemonic culture, complies with the belief systems upheld by the dominant paradigm, or values rationalization over intuition or other forms of knowing. The hierarchical lens is a delusion, however, because it does not allow us to see ourselves or one another clearly. Within the collective human psyche, the hierarchical framework or lens creates extreme and demoralizing pressure, competition, dislike, or hatred of that which is lower on the hierarchical scale.

Because hierarchy teaches that the higher you are on the hierarchical ladder, the better you are, we abandon our authenticity to try to fit in. We actively try to present our "best selves" and hide our weaknesses to maintain our place on the hierarchical scale. Participating on the treadmill of hierarchy and constant self-improvement to either maintain one's place or move higher up the scale is itself a full-time job that takes us further and further away from authentic power.

Hierarchy—and every *ism* that stems from this root—is a religion of *power over*, where power is defined as active force over another. Power is attained through exerting one's will and force onto the world. It is also attained through the approval given to some members of society and not others, as evidenced by systemic racism and classism. Within this hierarchical framework, some people are supported to succeed while others are not. Some are rewarded a title, position, wealth, or fame, while others are ignored, neglected, ostracized, or harmed. No one is authentically powerful within this paradigm because everyone is locked in a fear-based battle or competition. No one can ultimately feel secure.

The power-over framework that pervades our societies today cannot provide a path to genuine power because it is based on fear. The ultimate fear is ostracization. This framework disallows security for anyone on any rung of the ladder, high or low. Everyone—consciously or unconsciously—scans the barren landscape of comparison for external evidence to measure their place on the ladder. Forced to constantly evaluate how we are perceived and how we compare to others (superior/average/inferior), we also fear that we might drown or go unnoticed if we do not actively climb our way to the top. Even if we make it to the top, there is an ever-present burden of anxiety that we will somehow lose our position and fall. Therefore, there is no genuine satisfaction to anyone who participates in this belief system.

Humanity is exhausted and confused by the false messages of hierarchical perception, which carry thousands of years of momentum in human consciousness. In this external reward and punishment system, access to basic resources and having needs met are not givens but luxuries. The higher up on the hierarchy, the better off you will be. There is no way for humanity to survive, however, in the context of a paradigm that does not equally value every form of life at every level. We are relational beings, and shared power is the only kind of power that serves the whole. We exist on a planet of absolute interdependence. We can only win if everyone—and all forms of life—wins.

*   *   *

EXPERIENTIAL PRACTICE: THE BRAHMAVIHARAS AND LEARNING TO SEE EACH OTHER

One of my favorite partner practices to guide on retreat is called Learning to See Each Other. This practice was generated by Buddhist scholar and ecophilosopher Joanna Macy, one of my longtime teachers and mentors, as a way to teach the four Brahmaviharas. *It is a beautiful practice for seeing one another clearly, beyond the lens of hierarchical perception or labeling. The Brahmaviharas in Buddhism are the four abodes of the Buddha: loving-kindness, compassion,* mudita *or sympathetic joy, and equanimity. For the sake of this relational*

practice, interconnection is sometimes used in place of equanimity. I share this
practice directly from Joanna's book, Coming Back to Life.[5]

*Face your partner with eyes closed, remaining silent. Take a couple slow
breaths, centering yourself and exhaling tension. Open your eyes in soft
focus and look upon your partner's face. If you feel discomfort, just note it,
with patience and gentleness, and come back, when you can, and regard
your partner. You may never see this person again. The opportunity to
behold the uniqueness of this particular human being is given to you now.*

*To enter the first abode, open your awareness to the gifts and strengths
that are in this being. . . . Though you can only guess at them, there are
behind those eyes unmeasured reserves of courage and intelligence . . . of
patience, endurance, and wisdom. There are gifts there, of which even this
person is unaware. . . . Consider what these powers could do for the healing of your world if they were to be believed and acted on. As you consider
that, experience your desire that this person be free of fear. . . . Experience
how much you want this person to be released as well from greed, from
hatred and confusion, and from the causes of suffering. . . . Know that
what you are now experiencing is the great loving-kindness. . . . Closing
your eyes now, rest into your breathing . . .*

*Opening them again, we enter the second abode. Now, as you look
into those eyes, let yourself become aware of the pain that is there. There
are sorrows accumulated in that life, as in all human lives, though you
can only guess at them. There are disappointments and failures, losses
and loneliness and abuse. . . . There are hurts beyond the telling. . . . Let
yourself open to that pain, to hurts that this person may never have told
to another human being. . . . You cannot take that pain away, but you
can be with it. As you draw upon your capacity to be with your partner's
suffering, know that what you are experiencing is the great compassion. It
is very good for the healing of our world. . . .*

*Again, we close our eyes, opening them as we enter the third abode. As
you behold the person before you, consider how good it would be to work*

together on a joint project, toward a common goal. . . . What it would be like, taking risks together, conspiring together in zest and laughter, celebrating successes, consoling each other over the setbacks, forgiving each other when you make mistakes . . . and simply being there for each other. . . . As you open to that possibility, you open to the great wealth, the pleasure in each other's power, the joy in each other's joy. . . .

Now, entering the fourth and last abode, your eyes open, let your awareness drop deep within you like a stone, sinking below the level of what words can express . . . to the deep web of relationship that underlies all experience. . . . It is the web of life in which you have taken being and which interweaves us through all space and time. . . . See the being before you as if seeing the face of one who, at another time, place, was your lover or your enemy, your parent or your child. . . . And now you meet again on this brink of time almost as if by appointment. . . . And you know that your lives are as inextricably interwoven as nerve cells in the mind of a great being. . . . Out of that vast web you cannot fall. . . . No stupidity, or failure, or cowardice, can ever sever you from that living web. For that is what you are. . . . Rest in that knowing. Rest in the great peace. . . . Out of it we can act, we can risk anything. . . . And let every encounter be a homecoming to our true nature.

Holding the Brahmaviharas in our awareness in this way is a powerful expression of kalyana mitta, or spiritual friendship. It has the power to clear up great confusion between human beings. We can bring the spirit of this practice into any interaction we ever have.

Meeting One Another as the Mystery

When my husband and I prepared our wedding vows, we met with Joanna Macy and asked if she had any *encouragements* for the new phase of life we were embarking on. She suggested that we make a vow to remember to meet one another as the mystery. Think about what that means: meeting one another with the same quality of presence with which we would meet the mystery itself. For us, this has meant being committed to perceiving one another with openness, curiosity, and beginner's mind. We practice sensing into one another in each moment rather than assuming our partner is feeling the same way they were the day before. We practice acceptance and nonattachment regarding whatever state that person is in at the moment. This allows us to continually discover one another, continually fall in love with one another, and let one another be where they are, instead of needing to fit into our idea, expectation, or preference for what state they should be in. This also reminds us that one or the other is in continual process, flux, emergence, and evolution. When we meet the mystery, we do not assume that we already know all that there is to know. We can discover one another anew, over and over again.

The collective ramifications of this are great. In comparison, how often do we meet one another superficially with judgment and assumptions based on what we think we already know from previous experience?

We have all had the experience of being superficially evaluated and then categorized—based on one's race, class, appearance, employment, education, sexual orientation, or beliefs. We have all observed our own minds wanting to categorize other human beings. Even a seemingly casual experience of this kind of categorization can feel painful. Below is an experience that comes to mind for me personally.

Growing up in the liberal and wildly dynamic city of Los Angeles, I experienced the urban privilege of a diverse metropolitan area in which many shapes, colors, sizes, and expressions of the human family were visible around me every day. When I relocated to a small town in North Carolina, it was the first time I had ever lived in the middle of Southern culture where I did not necessarily visually fit in. I felt uncomfortable at times, surrounded by a more provincial and religious Christian culture with highly conservative beliefs. Appearing obviously Jewish and dressing more bohemian and individualistic than most women in the area, I sometimes experienced harsh looks that said, *You do not belong here!* Standing at 4' 11" next to my 6' 1" husband, I could tell we appeared as the odd couple to some. In turn, I sometimes observed myself quickly labeling strangers based on how they seemed to respond to me or even based on their looks. I had a tearful conversation with a close African American friend about my discomfort. As unsettling as it was to be treated as an outsider, I knew well that my friends of color had been treated as outsiders their entire lives and in far more dramatic ways.

Upon naming my discomfort out loud, I remembered to feel compassion for all parties involved in the habit of othering. I affirmed my practice to meet strangers as the mystery, anchored in cultural humility. Often, I found myself happily surprised at experiencing a more welcoming environment and new human connections. Of course, there is a difference between my experiences of being treated as an outsider and being physically beaten or brutalized because one is considered an outsider. There are varying degrees to which we might find the practice of meeting one another as the mystery applicable and beneficial.

Hierarchical perception is expensive. It keeps us locked in the illusion that we are separate from our human family. It keeps us rigidly and stubbornly protecting our version of what is correct and what is not against another's version rather than being willing to find the common ground required for evolution. Practice presents the possibility of meeting everyone as the mystery, with humility and beginner's mind.

Releasing the Lens of Me versus You: An Alternative to Polarizing Conversations

There have always been two side-by-side parallel patterns in human consciousness:

1. We are the superior people. If you appear different from us, you are "other" and a stranger.

2. We are all in this together. None of us would survive without each other.

Throughout history, we have embraced and taken the stranger into our homes. We have also reacted violently to and "othered" the stranger (viewed or treated them as intrinsically different from ourselves). I grew up hearing horrifying tales of the treatment of Jewish ancestors in the Russian pogroms and in the Holocaust, while also hearing phenomenal accounts of courageous people who risked their lives to protect and shelter Jewish families. My godmother shared remarkable stories from her childhood in Denmark, where her family sheltered Jews in the basement of their home. I also grew up hearing my grandfather's stories of his experiences during the Great Depression as a youth, which he spent as a hobo hopping trains across the continental United States seeking opportunities for work. While he often experienced great persecution due to his religious identity and economic status, he also shared heartwarming stories about the camaraderie, brotherhood, and long-lasting friendships created across racial and religious lines by men living as hobos during that time. He also never forgot the kind citizens who were willing to help shelter and feed them in times of need.

We all come from the same shared genetic history. It could be argued that everyone you will ever meet is in some distantly connected way your ancestral cousin, sister, brother, aunt, uncle, parent, or grandparent—albeit many times removed! For instance, genetics shows that regardless of race or ethnic background, all human beings carry 99.9 percent identical DNA. In terms of challenges we face today, how can we truly move our efforts to heal systemic racism going forward without looking deeply at our relationship to binary perception?

While race is natural, racism is not. Yet throughout history, the color of one's skin has provided the basis for a pattern of hierarchy and subjugation within cultures and governments that we still deal with today. In the words of Resmaa Menakem, the author of *My Grandmother's Hands*,

"The white body became the standardized, normal body; other bodies, especially Black bodies, were defined as aberrant or substandard."[6]

Since its inception, the United States has been built on systemic racism, and today we can see racial capitalism at play in everyday life. While there is critical work for each and every one of us, especially white-skinned people, to do to address the legacy of entrenched and systemic racism, a societal culture that fears confronting the dark shadows within us and without, even in our spiritual communities, can prevent us from having these vital conversations. We sometimes avoid facing the uncomfortable, complex, and messy conversations that are the only road that leads toward healing.

In the words of Ruth King, dharma teacher and author of *Mindful of Race: Transforming Racism from the Inside Out*, "Racism is a heart disease. How we think and respond is the core of racial suffering and racial healing. If we cannot think clearly and respond wisely, we will continue to damage the world's heart."[7]

I believe that we often stunt our capacity to have impactful conversations about healing the past because we continue to stand in "me versus you" consciousness and promote binary perception and polarization in how we converse. As a result, we dissect, analyze, and debate these highly sensitive issues—often with neither side willing to acknowledge our shared humanity. As we've seen in recent politics, there are also people interested in forms of xenophobia and white supremacy with which there is no moral middle. We create fields of judgment toward self and other rather than spaces that hold historical trauma with respect and love. We also show up to difficult conversations so defensive and so tightly holding on to our morally correct perspective that we close the door to collaborative healing. This model of polarization and "me versus you" does not help us to navigate collective healing. We can continue to converse solely from the mind of opinions, separation, and discrimination, or we can bring our hearts into conversations, in the moment, and allow a more emergent embodied kind of healing to occur. One of the keys is making the choice to continually expand our awareness to include we consciousness.

Showing Up for Difficult Conversations

In my experience, when we show up to difficult conversations anchored in body awareness, we bring more of our whole mind and heart to the table. This does not mean, in any way, negating the experience of those who have been marginalized. It is our collective responsibility to listen to those who are speaking to us, while also honoring and protecting the voices of the unseen and unheard. At the same time, if we continually interject *doer* and *done to*, perpetrator and victim, into every conversation about the negative *isms* we face today, we miss the opportunity to take responsibility for healing hierarchical perception and changing the paradigm completely.

As a white woman who is also a dharma teacher, I am continually deepening my capacity to stay present to racial complexity in conversations. Through honest and often uncomfortable communications, I continually deepen my awareness that I represent a racial group that has an impact on racial inequity and racial harmony. As we navigate our individual and shared experiences as members of a systemically racist society, it is important to anchor ourselves in compassion, patience, discomfort resiliency, forgiveness, and nonbinary perception. And it is most important that we find the space in our hearts to be uncomfortable together. A space created by two or more people committed to *shared presence* can hold everything, not just connection and ease. Shared presence is the unifying field that completely welcomes differing perspectives and difficult emotions. This is an important aspect of relational intelligence.

Entwined with racism, we are experiencing an unimaginable surge of hate crimes based upon religious intolerance within the United States and beyond. The history of religious intolerance has played out through genocides and religious wars around the globe, as demonstrated most recently through the Holocaust, and in Rwanda, Bosnia/Herzegovina, Cambodia, and Myanmar, to name a few of the atrocities humanity has witnessed.

The term *genocide* was coined in 1944 by Raphael Lemkin to mean the attempt to destroy an entire ethnic, religious, or racial group. *How We Get Along*, a two-year study done by the Woolf Institute in England and Wales, suggests that religion is the final frontier of personal prejudice. While most people interviewed had an evolving degree of racial acceptance, there was a line of hatred drawn against Muslims.[8]

It is vital that we create opportunities to acknowledge and feel together our shared human grief. It is important to move beyond symptomatic problem-solving to healing at the root. We have endless collective challenges to address. But all problems can be resolved in some way through seeing more clearly. All problems can become a gateway to opening our hearts beyond what we have imagined possible. Seeing with the heart allows us to move beyond the domain of "me or my beliefs" or "my position or opinion" as opposed to "you and your beliefs" or "your position or opinion." It allows us to have conversations that enable us to listen more openly to one another while welcoming difference. By doing so, we can experience great shifts in our consciousness together.

Whether we are having a potentially flammable and triggering conversation about politics or a bureaucratic conversation with a service representative on the phone, or we are engaged in working out a conflict with a family member, the world becomes a kinder place when we release the me-versus-you mentality. We are all conditioned with hierarchical perception, and we are each responsible for protecting life from the harm that hierarchical perception can cause.

In the words of Octavia Butler, "You are hierarchical. That's the older and more entrenched characteristic. We saw it in your closest animal relatives and in your most distant ones. It's a terrestrial characteristic. When human intelligence served it instead of guiding it, when human intelligence did not even acknowledge it as a problem but took pride in it or did not notice it at all. . . . That was like ignoring cancer."[9]

Notice how it feels in your body to take that statement in. Take in a deep, conscious breath and let go. Allow the impact of these powerful words to feed your heart's commitment to bringing awareness to the unconscious biases of hierarchical perception and learning to see from the heart.

From Humiliation to Humility

When we are willing to go beyond me versus you, we can experience and facilitate shared consciousness. *Facilitate* means "to make easier."[10] When we show up to relationship and leadership with we consciousness as our intention, we make the experience of unity more accessible to others. We consciousness is not a lofty idea. It does not discount our individual experience and differences. It simply invites us, as individuals, into the experience of shared presence.

We are all called to lead on behalf of what we love and the future we wish to cocreate. This is true whether we are in professional leadership positions or are parents, educators, activists, farmers, artists, or members of the human family hoping to leave the world a better place. The more we move beyond binary perception, the easier we can embrace a paradigm of leading with our whole selves. We can learn to *lead in the dark* and be *led by the dark.*

For a part of the psyche, nothing is more vulnerable than moving into a leadership position. Research has shown that fear of public speaking is one of the top three human fears. Through the framework of conditional love, a framework through which we often feel judged, we have all experienced moments in which we felt embarrassed or feared that we appeared stupid in front of a group. The dominant paradigm teaches, however, that leaders are not meant to experience doubt, fear, fragility, or make mistakes. A leader needs to present their best self all the time, correct? Leaders are, in essence, meant to transcend humanness. This is a faulty proposition.

We must also contend with a long legacy of spiritual teachers and wisdom keepers *sitting on a pedestal*, imparting wisdom to a group of people.

This old paradigm of leadership is rooted in hierarchy and expresses *power over* versus *power with*. It is rooted in duality, upholding the concept of perfection versus failure. As a result, people who might otherwise be motivated to step into leadership roles might instead refrain from doing so, due to the pressure and fear of humiliation perpetuated by this hierarchical model.

There is a popular notion in today's world that a leader is someone who has attained a strong, sturdy level of confidence and charisma. A leader has no room for uncertainty, doubt, a wrong turn, or even a simple mistake. The idea is that success, similar to spiritual enlightenment, is to attain a perfect state. You are either 100 percent successful as a leader or must be considered deficient and a failure.

Collective conditioning has taught us that if the force carrying you forward into the known is not based upon supreme confidence, then you ought not to move. Endarkenment offers a different perspective. We all fall sometimes. We all fail at meeting often artificial or unrealistic standards. We all disappoint at times, both ourselves and others. Genuine leadership has nothing to do with supreme confidence or perfection. It has to do with presence, courage, fierce compassion, and vulnerability.

In my own experience, I began suffering from symptoms of Lyme disease simultaneously with evolving in my leadership role. With Lyme, I often felt my worst and never knew from one day to the next if I would be in a stronger or weaker physical state. I sometimes experienced *word drop*, the loss of access to the word I was just about to say. I often felt physically fragile, while feeling spiritually enlivened.

My old conditioning might have motivated me to hide behind a false facade. But having spent years of my life meditating by that time, I trusted in my ability to be present. I trusted my heart, and I was willing to trust the mystery to guide me. In other words, I was willing to risk humiliation in order to affirm my embodiment of absolute humility. This was, and continues to be, one of the greatest sources of liberation in my life. It is the freedom of surrendering our often-false standards in order to allow us to model what is possible beyond those standards. It is the freedom to allow ourselves to be seen as we are. It is the freedom from fear of failure.

Leading in the dark is a path of freedom from *small self.* My courage came from my desire to be of genuine service. Every time I showed up with courage, often alongside fear, I experienced transformation. Letting go of my agenda meant both letting go of a set, planned, and scripted course for any teaching and letting go of concerns regarding my personal presentation while teaching. The focus was on the subtle energy and multidimensional field of the group I was leading, rather than on anything having to do with me. My entire path became one of learning and teaching the art of leadership through letting go of the small self.

It is a subversive act in today's world to accept ourselves as we already are. We can spend our entire lifetime striving constantly to improve ourselves, while consuming the capitalistic message of inadequacy—or we can arrive. When we show up in complete self-acceptance, we give others permission to do the same. Self-acceptance can be contagious.

Authentic leadership means to show up naked. Without a shield or sword, without a script or plan, we can allow our relationships to be about transformation rather than proving ourselves. Instead of seeking approval from others, we can receive it directly from ourselves. Instead of trying to improve ourselves to get to "okayness," we can go directly to *okayness.* We can acknowledge that judgment is the only thing in our way. We can also begin to realize that we are not the hero achieving the grail. We are the obstruction.

Getting Out of the Way

For me, endarkenment is about emptying myself and letting go of my personal agenda to be a vessel for more. The traits I reawakened through endarkenment, such as receptivity, deep listening, commitment to process over product, inquiry into the moment, emergence, and reverence for the unknown, have informed my entire way of living. The impact affirmed my trust not in the confidence in separate self but in the shared presence we channel when we get out of the way. Through this consciousness, we can allow every individual in a group field, or whomever we are talking with, to be met where they are. As leaders, we can invite people to grow or evolve in exactly the way they are ready for—not through our own agenda for them but through deeply listening to them. We can offer ourselves in spiritual friendship, or *kalyana mitta*.

Genuine humility is not about trading in self-aggrandizement for self-deprecation. It is not about hiding our gifts from others. Genuine humility is freeing one's self from both self-aggrandizement and self-deprecation. It is about moving beyond the self as our domain and, instead, offering ourselves in service to the whole. This is a powerful expression of leadership, but it is completely vulnerable at the same time. This whole we care for, of course, also includes our individual self.

When we lead by letting go of ego and the *small self*, we learn to trust life to take us where we need to go. There is nothing more powerful than trusting life. By so doing, we achieve the following:

1. **Liberation from the idea of success as binary.** There is both success and failure and, for anyone committed to growth, they sometimes overlap or exist at the same time.
2. **Liberation from the idea of success as a by-product of our efforts.** We enter instead into the emergent, joyful, encircling, and life-affirming experience of the process itself as success.

It is then that something quite extraordinary becomes attainable: we are able to model for others the magic of letting go and trusting life to lead us.

Intimacy Arises from Empty Space

In the fall of 2013, I led another weeklong meditation retreat in Ojai, California. On the final night of this retreat, I spoke openly and honestly about my journey with Lyme and the dharma teachings I had harvested. I was, by that time, in much better physical health than I had been and felt the potential for a new chapter to open up in my life. At the end of my talk, I shared that, on a personal level, feeling immeasurable joy to be in a well body again, I envisioned spending a lot of time dancing. I also expressed a hope and readiness to meet my life partner. Partnership and romance had, at times, felt challenging, while navigating the ups and downs of Lyme.

Later that night, I experienced a powerful dream in which I was instructed to move to Ojai—that it was important that the land and community of Ojai become my home base. I saw myself in perfect harmony with the land of Ojai. My ancestors had lived in Ojai, but I had only spent time there on retreat. I woke up somewhat confused, as I was living in Portland, Oregon, at the time and establishing my life there. That same morning, however, I received a surprising message from my landlord announcing that he was selling the house where I rented a room in a collective household. One hour later, I received a synchronistic text from a close friend in Ojai, out of the blue, asking if I might be available to house-sit for a few months and take care of her cat and garden. In a series of swift and unexpected communications, within twenty-four hours, life completely realigned itself for me to move to Ojai.

On my first day there, walking down the street, I saw an ad for a conscious dance gathering that would take place that night. I reached out to a couple of girlfriends and invited them to join me. The man facilitating the gathering was Mark . . . a warm, gentle, gorgeous being with a great sense of humor, with whom I felt an immediate resonance.

The first time we sat down together, to share a meal and get to know one another, we both experienced a natural and surprising degree of ease, settledness, and delight in each other's presence. After sitting and talking in a field in which time dissolved, Mark shared, "Wow! Being with you feels more spacious than anyone I have spent time with." By meeting one another empty rather than full of agenda or effort, not trying to impress one another, we got to sense into one another's essence. Two months after our first meeting, we acknowledged that we had fallen in love. We recognized that we belonged with each other—not *to* each other, but *with* each other. I realized that my dream had guided me off my planned course directly to Mark. Our initial meeting blossomed into the most vital love partnership of my life, and some years later, we were married.

* * *

MINDFUL INQUIRY

For some of you, the practice of showing up as you are, in vulnerability, is central to your life. For others, it may sound scary. Can you think of a time that allowing yourself to be seen, exactly as you are, brought more genuine connection? What about a time someone was willing to show up for you in true vulnerability?

Where has hierarchical perception gotten in the way of how you perceive another human being or a group of humans? Where have the labels good/bad, light/dark, positive/negative, higher/lower, better/worse gotten in the way of clear seeing? Please notice how it feels in your body to reflect on these questions and practice self-compassion.

Now consider this: How have you been othered through hierarchical perception? Notice how it feels in your body to reflect on these questions and practice self-compassion. Consider making a list of instances that stand out in your life. Notice which of these still trigger you and which have been healed or forgiven. Bring care and self-compassion to this inquiry.

* * *

EXPERIENTIAL PRACTICE: THE TAO IN EVERYDAY LIFE

As shared in this chapter, the ancient Tao beautifully illustrates the whole of the yin and yang and captures the complete absence of polarization in life. For this practice, allow yourself, over the course of twenty-four hours, to pay attention to evidence of the whole of yin and yang curled around each other, throughout your human experience. Without categorizing life as good/bad, light/dark, positive/negative, right/wrong, how does your awareness expand to a greater sense of wholeness and inclusivity? Rather than labeling your experiences as positive/negative, notice what happens when you instead inquire, "How am I experiencing the full spectrum of light and dark, yin and yang? How do I experience the light in the dark and the dark in the light? How does this awareness expand my recognition of the sacred? Record any observations and reflections on a fresh page in your journal.

9

Dreams, Possibility, and Moral Imagination

The Role of the Invisible Realm in Awakening

As you enter positions of trust and power, dream a little before you think.

TONI MORRISON[1]

THE INVISIBLE REALM IS REAL. We can step into it through deep meditation, shamanic journeying, nocturnal dreams, and even by theta brainwave induction as we rest in suspended fascination with the leaves of a tree. We can access it through conscious movement practice or the creative use of our imagination and subconscious mind. It is often referred to as the spirit world, but it is also called "the place of non-where" by the Persians, the "otherworld" by Celts, "dreamtime" by Australian Aborigines, and "the lower, middle, and upper world" in many shamanic traditions. Because our everyday sensory life is experienced physically, in three dimensions, and the imaginal realm is not physical, it is often discounted. Through a restrictive cultural pattern, this essential aspect of human existence is labeled "fantasy" and has no practical purpose aside from a billion-dollar entertainment industry.

To enter any conversation about darkness and dreaming in which we are both asleep and awake to the mystery, there must be a recognition, even if just a glimmer, of the reality of the invisible realm. In actuality, spiritual practice teaches us that if we want to see clearly and access reality, we must go beyond the assumed reality of mental/physical existence and also experience the invisible.

We learn through meditation practice that our ever-changing thoughts and emotions are not reality. We learn that what we see visually is not reality. We learn to access the 360-degree awareness that expands our perception—physically and energetically—beyond the conditioned mind as primary orientation, to consciousness itself.

Taking Responsibility for Our Collective Imagination

We each contribute to the morphic field—the shared memory field of human consciousness—through our imagination. When we get lost in the conditioned mind, ruminate about the past or future, or project onto one another, we are unconsciously exercising our imagination. Through the music and books we take in, the movies and TV shows we create and view, the ideas and biases we put out into the world, we feed our collective story.

The quality of our life experience is determined by the focus of our attention. That which we give our attention to grows. Therefore, life manifests for us the storylines or realities that we click on. We contribute regularly to our collective future by imagining—without being aware of the possible longer-term impact doing so may have. Our negative judgment toward someone can become a detrimental curse, just as our well wishes toward another can offer a palpable blessing.

We can use our waking and sleeping dreams to either incubate the desires of our shared heart and what we know is possible for humanity or to further the myth of separation.

Research by Fredric Jameson showed that it is easier for human beings to imagine an end to the world than an end to capitalism.[2] I find this astounding and illustrative of the case of mistaken identity humanity is caught up in. While we have all the technology needed to go beyond fossil-fuel reliance, we have found it hard to imagine a world that operates through renewable energy. We have not been willing to imagine food security beyond conventional agribusiness, though regenerative agriculture offers both a means for sustainable food production and for slowing climate change. When we don't dream our dreams, we are left to fit ourselves into the tiny pages of existing stories, even if they cause harm.

It is the nature of the conditioned mind to scan for perceived limitations. This process creates outer forms that match those limitations. The visionary heart stands in possibility. It grows, evolves, and refines our inner and outer world to align with the possibilities. A life-affirming dream, for instance, can transform us from the inside out. It will demand that we release limiting beliefs and energy-draining habits and perhaps develop or uncover the discipline and courage needed to bring our dream into fruition. Spirit and matter work in collaboration, bending and transforming externals in direct correlation with our willingness to bend and open our minds. Spirit informs matter and matter responds.

Dreamtime as a Doorway to the Great Self

In the words of the cultural historian Thomas Berry, "The universe must be experienced as the Great Self. Each is fulfilled in the other: the Great Self is fulfilled in the individual self, and the individual self is fulfilled in the Great Self. Alienation is overcome as soon as we experience this surge of energy from the source that has brought the universe through the centuries. New fields of energy become available to support the human venture."[3]

Life presents abundant doorways to experience the Great Self in every moment of our lives. One of these doorways is dreaming. There are so many living beings, ancestors, and other forms of life who want to dream with us and help us remember more. Woven into our sleep cycles are the nocturnal dreams that connect us to information from beyond.

Perhaps the first human experience of seeing in the dark was a nocturnal dream. We have forever surrendered our bodies to deep sleep and, enveloped by this restorative state, we have received illumination and vision. We have given ourselves to the oceanic tides of the dark forever . . . reveling in the communications of the subconscious.

While the dominant paradigm perceives imagination as fantasy, the imaginal world has been an essential and foundational aspect of the human experience throughout all of history. Many ancient civilizations and present-day indigenous cultures have celebrated communion with the invisible realm through nocturnal dreams. While the dominant paradigm does not tend to make ample provision for deep sleep, there are spiritual traditions across the planet that consider sleep and dreamtime the most important time of day.

Dreamtime, or dreaming, for Australian Aboriginal people represents the time when the spirits of the ancestors visit the land. The ancestors, in dreamtime, create new life and form important physical geographic sites and formations.[4]

In the Peruvian Amazon tradition of the Sonenekuiñaji peoples, a multinatural perspectivism is accessed in dreams that guide their daily life. They experience *eshawa*, a phenomenon explained as a blurring and integrating of dreaming and waking realities. This gives all animate beings a dimension of personhood. It gives the Sonenekuiñaji people the ability to gain knowledge and understanding through the dream narratives of many forms of life. These peoples turn to dreams for access to literal, metaphorical, and prophetic sources of information. They dream of plants to cure sickness and they dream of where to find food.

The Chipewyan people, indigenous to Northern Canada, hold a monistic worldview, where spiritual and physical reality exists as one. They exist in an intercommunicative relationship with animals who help them to obtain their practical knowledge of the bush sensibilities. This comes to them through dreams and guides them through their daily life. In their worldview, all life forms "are inextricably engaged in a complex communicative interrelationship."[5]

Conscious engagement with dreams is also woven into many European traditions. An example is the Gaelic poet, who was considered a mystic created in partnership with darkness. In the dark and through dreams, the Gaelic poet sensed the light of inspiration. Darkness was the muse from which inspiration arose. According to an account from 1722, the typical poet lay in an unlit hut working out his verses "upon his own bed in the dark." The Gaelic poet was viewed as a deeply shamanic figure bestowed with many of the same skills and responsibilities, which could include word doctoring, divination, blessing, and cursing.[6]

Discounting Dreams and the Dreamer

Although we spend half our lives in nighttime dreaming, within the paradigm of rationalization, anthropocentricity, and technology in the modern world, it is easy to discount the domain of dreams. Tibetan Buddhist Andrew Holecek, who teaches nocturnal meditation and dream yoga, suggests that we resist the cocreative opportunity of dreaming because we are so attached to wake-centricity, the conscious mind, and the domain of daylight. We prefer the linear rational mind to the dreamscape of liminality. We tend to push things away that dreams reveal in the subconscious and bring to the surface.[7] Through hierarchical perception we discount dreaming and tell ourselves the following instead:

Logic is superior to imagination.
Cognitive understanding is better than intuition.
Human cleverness is superior to partnership with nature.

Being centered and mindful is separate from being imaginative or
dreamy.

Even within Zen Buddhism, there can be an unconscious bias that pits
realization over imagination. The open and soft qualities of attunement
and intuition can be perceived to be in service to something harder and
brighter: realization. There can also be a duality of "centered" versus "not
centered." Centered is deemed superior, while not centered can be perceived as flaky or *woo-woo*. The term *woo-woo* is commonly used to refer
to "unconventional things not grounded in science."

This is paradoxical. Nothing could be more centered than cultivating
and applying intuition, imagination, and relational forms of knowing. It is
our nature to pay attention in the moment and to be responsive to life as
it is arising. Practice teaches us to allow our emergent collaboration with
life to be our present-moment orientation.

Honoring Nocturnal Dreams

My grandmother Clare—my mother's mother—taught me, as a young girl,
to honor my nighttime dreams, as her grandmother had taught her. Some
dreams are messengers, she shared. Some dreams are mirrors with useful information to help you know yourself. Some dreams are connectors,
with the potential to connect you with all beings in your heart. And some
dreams have guidance to offer you.

My grandmother was an artist, educator, and Jungian dream therapist
who reflected on and recorded all of her dreams. She used oil paints and
watercolor to paint her dreams and integrate their messages. I recognized
my grandmother as a wise elder, a grounded woman who was also a vol-
cano of unbridled creativity. She was a free spirit with a huge appetite for
play and zest for life. My grandmother was a visionary, who founded a
school and educational curriculum for children based on creativity and

the arts. She fueled some of the pain from her own life's trauma into dreaming a visionary education based on creative expression.

My grandmother Clare was also a deep listener who provided a safe place for emotional awareness. Growing up, she gently encouraged me to listen to my dreams and pay attention to the sacred messages my dreams carried. She encouraged me to receive dreams without intellectually analyzing them and to listen for myself. She suggested that I pose questions into the realm of dreams. My grandmother also spoke of not being superstitious about dreams but simply being open to the deep well of information available in the night.

Years later, after my grandmother passed away when I was sixteen, she visited me often in my dreams. My grandmother's encouragement gifted me a foundation for a self-guided dream practice throughout my life. In every phase of this life—which has been a metaphorical walk through the dark—dreams, intuition, and conscious use of the imaginal realm have been my greatest allies. Dreams have served me in the domain of healing, spiritual growth, relationships, navigating uncertainty, deepening my connection with the natural and invisible world, and guiding my desire to be of service. These aspects of life have all been directed by my dreamworld. I have also worked consciously with nightmares over the years, allowing nocturnal meditation practices to support me in the healing of trauma arising in the night.

Many spiritual traditions recognize the nighttime as the domain of ancestors and spirits. Working with dreams can open us up to information from these realms, which speak to us through precognitive symbols, poetry, mythology, imagery, and metaphor. There exist many skillful guides to dreamwork in today's world, from dream yoga and lucid dreaming to shamanic practices and collective dreaming. There are five aspects of dreamwork that I find especially useful and accessible to many:

1. Emotional and spiritual integration and metabolization
2. Connection to nature through pattern language

3. Connection to loved ones and ancestors across time and space
4. Working with the subconscious and healing trauma
5. Guidance and direction from spirit

Emotional and Spiritual Integration and Metabolism

Nocturnal dreams allow for emotional relevancy and emotional truth to be experienced without imposition. During the day, it can be easy to identify our emotions in an often-self-fulfilling way. Assuming that we must have a reason to feel the way we do, we attempt to identify that reason. *I don't know why I'm feeling this sadness today. Something must be wrong.* We attempt to *understand* our experience, rather than *feel* our experience.

Trying to understand or make sense of a feeling disallows an emotion to exist and express itself in the all-inclusive field of being. Alternatively, the dreamer can offer the waking human emotional content free of the framework of emotions that are categorized when we are awake.

I believe that dreams can help us to process our pain for our world. Integrating the heartbreak, for instance, of witnessing climate change and species extinction unfolding at a faster pace than even scientists expected is not something we can emotionally digest through rationalization or analysis. Dreaming, like meditating and journeying into the subconscious, gives our pain a field beyond words to metabolize, integrate, and bring into wholeness.

Connection to Nature through Pattern Language

Throughout my adult life, I've been aware of profound communication with the natural world through dreams. I've had enough unique experiences to know that we dream at night not in isolation but with the land, the creatures, the plants, and the many forms of life that make up the web of coexistence. I have had enough outside-the-box experience with patterns in dreams to suspect that the dreamer can go into complex systems without a logical excuse to do so. From physical systems of the body to ecosystems, I've become curious about the dreamer's capacity to enter and communicate with systems with an intelligence that goes beyond what we've been conditioned to expect or understand.

The first time I noticed that nature could speak to me through dreams in a different way than I experienced during my waking hours, I was operating an organic farm and CSA (community supported agriculture) in Arizona. Working with the soil and plants intimately throughout the day, I was in constant communication with the plants, insects, seeds, and soil. I slowly became aware that our interactions were extending into the night, every night. My dreams would play out patterns within the plants, patterns within the soil, patterns of the interplay of sunlight and shade, patterns within the orchards I had pruned, and even patterns within the entire farm. Sometimes the patterns communicated with me, telling me when it was time to sow a seed or plant a companion crop. Sometimes these patterns just brought deeper connectedness with the farm. Because farming is a full-time job, and I gave my body-mind so intimately to this farm, I was not surprised by the relationship I had with the plants in dreamtime. It made me more aware of the potential for communication with the world of plants, specifically, that humans can foster when we open our hearts to this.

Years later, when I had the opportunity to spend the summer living on an island, swimming daily in the ocean, I became aware of the patterns of ocean water speaking to me through my nighttime dreams. I reveled in the enjoyment of these patterns and sometimes woke up with a sense of what the nature of the tides might be on that day. I spent that summer not swimming just for enjoyment but swimming as a practice of listening to the water element. In one of my dreams, I was shown the whereabouts of a large sea turtle who inhabited the cove I swam in each day. The following morning, curious if my dream held relevance, I swam out to that exact spot and was amazed to find that, indeed, the giant sea turtle awaited me.

Today, I am married to a healer who makes medicine from flower essences. I became aware early on in our relationship that he exists in constant collaboration and communication with the world of flowers. When we hike together, he will receive a calling that takes us a quarter mile off trail, unexpectedly directing us to a rare flower he had hoped to find. Flowers also speak to him in dreams, offering further insight into his daytime research and into the medicine of the flower essences he makes. While my husband has a unique gift, I believe that everyone has the capacity for multinatural awareness, and it can be tapped into through the quality with which we pay attention.

Connection to Loved Ones and Ancestors Across Time and Space

Through conversations with the community I serve, I have learned that one of the most accessible aspects of dreaming is communication with loved ones. Sometimes we can brush these communications off as inexplicable or rare, but my experience has been that dreamtime is the domain for crystal-clear communication with all beings we hold a heart connection to. Having lost, by the age of twenty, many people who were important to me, including my father, aunts, uncle, and grandparents, I received confirmation at a young age that connection with loved ones continues beyond physicality, time, and space.

As a monastic, I learned to trust that important communications would arrive through my dreams, in both gentle and more direct ways. One summer night, I dreamt that I was sitting in a wooden cabin by a hearth fire with a mentor I had not spoken with in months. In this dream we were having our last conversation before they died. The tone of the dream was warm and simultaneously communicated that the contents of our conversation carried great importance. The dream inspired me to reach out to this friend, only to learn that, on the day of my dream, they had experienced the greatest trauma of their life. It had left them feeling alone, scared, and praying for support. The ensuing conversations we had brought the needed support, and for the first time, in a way I could not have foreseen, our relationship transformed from one of mentee/mentor to one of reciprocity. A new level of intimacy, trust, and mutuality was birthed in a relationship I valued deeply.

Working with the Subconscious and Healing Trauma

There are many pathways for working with the subconscious through dreams for healing trauma and difficult emotions, including lucid dreaming and dream yoga. When we make a more conscious link between the domain of sleep/dreams and our waking consciousness, doorways for healing can open. I first realized that dreams were a vital ground for healing trauma while living as a monastic. In the first couple of months at the monastery, I had nightmares every single night, as if experiencing a psychic detox. Although the nature of these dreams showed me that the imprint of trauma from my past was finally being given space to arise, it was a frightening and depleting experience. At the same time, through the inner work I was doing during the day, I understood that compassion was the most important component for releasing emotional patterns held in my subconscious. Inspired by my daytime practice, I made a recording of my own compassionate voice, offering genuine reassurance, encouragement, and loving-kindness. This was not at all the voice of a cheerleader or someone trying to fix/solve my pain. Rather, this voice was the wise compassionate presence I accessed through stillness. This steadfast companion spoke words of truth that soothed me and was willing to stay present with me no matter what I encountered or experienced. I began listening to the recording before falling asleep, curious to see what would happen. One night, I woke up at midnight from a nightmare and immediately put on my headphones to listen to the recording. This became a regular practice. A week later, I awoke in my dream to the voice of self-compassion entering during a nightmare. The entire context of the dream shifted and, the next night, I set the intention to bring more intention to taking an active role/ choice in dreams. From then on, I began practicing self-compassion within my dreamscapes. While it was not immediate, my repetitive nightmares ceased. My empowerment to work actively with my dreamworld was taken to a new level that continues to evolve and promote healing to this day.

Guidance and Direction from Spirit

In this age of global uncertainty, one of the capacities we all need to develop is our *earth attunement*. Like every living animal, we are designed to be attuned to the weather, the land we inhabit, and climate. In an age of wild and unexpected change, I suspect that our dreamworld can help us to sense emergent change and respond more wisely through attunement and adaptation.

The name Ojai comes from the Chumash word for *nest*. Surrounded by stunning mountains, manzanitas, orange groves, and a wild chaparral landscape, it was, indeed, a lovely "nest" for my relationship with Mark to deepen. We rented a tiny four-hundred-square-foot cottage in someone's garden that we called *The House of Birds*.

While Ojai was an extremely privileged place to live and allowed us access to the wilderness while we offered our work in Los Angeles and beyond, the Southern California drought continued to worsen during our time there. Taking our morning walk along a beautiful dried-up riverbed, we witnessed the slow deaths of tree after tree and a nearby lake diminishing every month. We did not see the community rallying in efforts to innovate a drought-tolerant lifestyle. Through our disappointment and the negative impact of the heat on our health, we began to seek an alternative place to call home and build our future.

Together we envisioned stewarding land one day but could not imagine having the resources to buy a home, particularly in California, where housing prices had skyrocketed. We nevertheless held on to the idea as a possibility in the future.

As we began searching for a solution, I dreamt one night about Black Mountain, North Carolina, a small town nestled in foothills that I had visited twenty years earlier. I remembered this place as a hearth of temperate green forests, wild mushrooms, biodiversity, and flowing water. This was a small mountain town that still moved at a comparatively slow pace. We visited Black Mountain together soon after in 2016, when I was invited to lead a retreat nearby, and we knew immediately that we could set up our lives there. Through synchronicity, we learned about a small house in an ecovillage outside Black Mountain and arranged to rent it, without even seeing it. The house was called The Nest, and we knew immediately that it was meant to be ours.

We now knew where to go but moving across the country felt intimidating. In fact, we found ourselves dragging our feet. Then in October 2017, a message arrived loud and clear through another dream—telling us it was time to exit Ojai. A month later, we drove across the country over nine days, pulling a heavy load of belongings. We drove slowly and leisurely, savoring the journey to a new life. As soon as we had unpacked and settled into our new space, however, we received the heartbreaking news from friends: Ojai was on fire. Exactly one month and one day after we had left Ojai, the place we had called home together for four years was hit by one of the most devastating fires that California had ever seen.

The Move to North Carolina: Being Open to Magic

Mark and I lived happily in Black Mountain for three years before finding the land and long-term home we had dreamed of stewarding. In January 2020, just before the COVID-19 pandemic began, we sat down one evening by candlelight to create a list of everything we hoped to manifest in our dream home. We took the colored markers out from our chest of art supplies and took turns visioning together: affordability, south-facing flat garden space, spring water, a creek. We posted this list by our home altar and read it aloud from time to time, feeling the resonance of knowing clearly what we wanted to call in.

We did not know if our vision existed at a price we could afford, but we were open to a little bit of magic. Although we periodically looked through real estate listings, another year went by. One night, Mark intuitively brought out our list to reactivate it. I read it over and added one more detail to our vision: a charming home office next to a creek, painted red. I have always loved the color red and find comfort and warmth in rooms painted red.

That night I had a dream in which each of our late fathers helped us to find this house. The following morning, my husband received a notice in his inbox about a house newly on the market, up the mountain road from where we then lived. We made an appointment after work and were delighted to find that every single detail on our list was met. As we wandered through this home, the last room we came to was a beautiful and charming red office next to the small creek that meandered through the land.

We went home, wrote a personal letter, and pressed the send button. We then turned off our phones and went on a walk, resting in the field of possibility while letting go at the same time. Anything could happen. At the end of our walk, we turned our phones back on and learned that our offer had been immediately accepted! Within three weeks we had the keys to our new dream home.

Consciously Using Our Imagination

In my life, nothing of meaning—from my spiritual practice to teaching and being of service, from my marriage and friendship and the sangha I guide to my physical healing process—would have been possible without a commitment to releasing the mind from limitation. Throughout my entire healing process and to this day, I have engaged consciously with the imaginal realm through active imagination to help my body remember how it feels to thrive physically. I have used radical imagination to remember the pulse and pleasure of activities my body was physically unable to do. I have relied upon conscious use of the imagination to imagine courageous action in the face of paralyzing fear.

In his research about the power of visionary states, Alan Richardson instructed one group of school children to throw basketball each day for twenty days. He asked another group of school children to visualize making perfect shots into the hoop for twenty days, without actually physically throwing the ball. His research showed that after twenty days, the first group showed a 24 percent improvement. The second group, without even having picked up one ball, showed a 23 percent improvement.[8]

My understanding of dream states and the imaginal realm is that this is the domain of interdependence and possibility. The language of dreams extends beyond the human mind to *big mind*—the mind of creation. Practice is creating the world we choose to live in moment by moment. Dreaming allows us to imagine what we may have perceived as impossible and open toward new possibility.

The Work That Reconnects is a field of work created by Joanna Macy for deepening our embodiment of interconnection and transforming our pain for our world into compassionate action. Within the Work That Reconnects process, we actively exercise our imagination to open new pathways for conscious response to our world. We courageously and playfully engage the imagination in order to bend the mind of limitation and see with new eyes. We dream of ways we might be of greater service to our world and ways we might powerfully collaborate. We stretch our minds and hearts in order to feel, see, and sense ourselves taking action from the courage in our hearts.

When guiding organizations to create fresh vision and conscious intention, I invite people to playfully dream together, in journeys taken far beyond the rational mind. When I guide couples in transformative work, I invite them often to share meaningful past and creative future memories with one another. The active use of imagining together inspires and unlocks their understanding of what brought them together. It reminds them of their passion and their heart's desire to heal.

The Courage to Dream and Imagine

For years, my mother had this quote on her desk: "People who say it cannot be done should not interrupt those who are doing it!" Perhaps the most empowering gift and privilege I received from my upbringing was my family's commitment to creative imagination. The family I grew up in carries a legacy of artists, visionaries, poets, and change agents. Our home was a creativity workshop, as the homes of my mother, sister and brothers, and my extended family continue to be to this day. In my family, to step outside the box in rebellion to the status quo was rewarded, which was a unique paradigm to live within. Although my family did not come from money, the resources of imagination, audacity, generosity, and creative response were abundant. I witnessed my family and extended family fuel their pain for our world into dreams of a better one. This, along with my white privilege—although for a long time I did not realize it—afforded the sense that my voice and dreams mattered. I do not take these privileges for granted today. Those of us who are privileged in any way have a moral responsibility to help the collective to dream a more life-affirming dream.

Some Dreams Don't Come True

In 1981, my mother met Bobby, an angry twelve-year-old African American boy, in Skid Row where he lived with his single mother and siblings in a transient hotel. It was a horrible environment for children, their lives surrounded by violence, crime, and debris-strewn alleyways and vacant lots. After Bobby's family moved back to South Central Los Angeles, my mother lost track of him. Twenty years later, she learned the following: In 1986, at age sixteen, Bobby was arrested for violent crimes that he did not commit. Tried in adult court, he was wrongfully convicted of five felonies and given a term of twenty-five years to life. Finally released in 2004 after eighteen years, he sought out my mother for help and guidance.

As they reconnected, my mom was struck by what a warm, hopeful, deeply intelligent young man Bobby had become. His many travesties had helped him to evolve exponentially. Over the next two years, Bobby rebuilt his life and was about to begin a full-time job, when he was arrested for a trumped-up parole violation (registration of a faulty address). Rather than accept a plea bargain of six years and sure of his innocence, Bobby chose to go before a judge. Informed of his earlier convictions—which at the time constituted two strikes—the jury deemed him guilty. My mother sat in the courthouse astonished, as Bobby was sentenced to a second twenty-five-years-to-life term under the California "three strikes" law and was led away.

Throughout this second incarceration, as the appeals process slowly moved forward and then failed, Bobby maintained a commitment to consciously dreaming of his future. He recognized the pain of his fellow inmates and dreamed of stepping into leadership for young Black men who were struggling with the psychological traumas of entrenched poverty, racism, and injustice. Bobby held on to his dreams as a lifeline and formed himself into the person who could manifest them. He spoke more eloquently and with more conviction about his dream of being of service than most people I have ever known. But he never had the opportunity to actualize his dreams. In February 2020, as pro bono attorneys were finally reviewing his case, Bobby was mistreated by prison guards, leaving him with irreversible brain damage and semicomatose. The possibilities Bobby dreamed of had been squashed by the collective dream of systemic racism, which views people like Bobby—with his huge heart and kind spirit—as menaces to society who need to be punished and locked away. Sometimes dreams come true, and sometimes they do not.

We can create a new collective dream that serves compassion, equity, and love, or we can continue to dream a collective dream that serves hierarchy, hatred, and othering. We are each required to take responsibility for the direction of our collective imagination.

Moral Imagination

Our collective stories, while having fed generations of limiting beliefs, are not who we are. In this time of change, courageously using our creative imagination on behalf of the whole is perhaps the most important practice there is. Collective transformation lives in our willingness to dream more life-affirming dreams than we have before—and to dream not on our own behalf, but on life's behalf.

Theologian Martin Buber coined the term *moral imagination*.[9] Moral imagination points to the importance of actively engaging our imaginations together, on behalf of the collective. There is a responsibility to our collective, as an example, to actively imagine a world beyond racism. *How would this world look and feel? How would a world in which we responded consciously and courageously to climate change and species extinction look? How would a skillful response look if we were willing to dream larger? What happens when we dream with and on behalf of the web of interdependence and ask life to show us something more?*

In the words of Thomas Berry, "We are not lacking in the dynamic forces needed to create the future. We live immersed in a sea of energy beyond all comprehension."[10] The conscious use of our imaginal faculties in service to life does not require that we exit the moment. It is when we are present, with an open mind and open heart, that we can reach into greater possibility. While everything in the outer world is disturbed and shifting due to the agitation and disruption in our collective field, it is essential that people recognize, validate, cultivate, and learn to apply the strength of their imaginal faculties. This is how we can bring ourselves home to what is real.

Maya and the Illusory Nature of Reality

It is up to each of us to see beyond the seemingly set-in-stone assumptions that the mind of limitation insists upon. The *bodhisattva* engaged in the world is responsible for maintaining awareness of fluidity and conscious choice within what appears to be solid. This requires letting go of habit, of passive consumption, and our investment in collective limiting beliefs. It involves becoming a steward of one's attention and imagination, in order to offer oneself in stewardship to life.

In Buddhist philosophy, it is understood that all of life is a dream, whether we are waking or sleeping. In other words, it is *maya*, illusion. Just a dream. Maya in Hindu and Buddhist philosophy points to the limited, purely mental and physical reality in which our everyday consciousness has become entangled. While many of us were taught that what we see is reality, this is in fact not true. Maya veils our true unified self. Meditation allows us to recognize the illusory nature of reality or the dreaming nature of existence. Within every field we visually see that appears to be "real" and "set in stone," there also exists limitless possibility. *Darkness is the field of unformed possibility before we choose a limited form.*

If we embrace the radical attitude of the dreamer, the explorer, the detective, the artist, the visionary, and the pioneer in our practice, we can integrate dreaming into our awakening consciousness. Practice asks us to continually look behind the veil of ordinary reality and investigate our actual experience—and then to discern truth from delusion. We learn to recognize what our consciousness is bringing to each moment. We learn to see the dramas and contractions created by the separate self, from an open-minded and open-hearted perception. We begin to realize that we are not limited to the manuals we have been given.

One of the major opportunities available to humans is the unification of the waking dream and the sleeping dream. Through dreaming consciously, we can step aside from what we have been told to be and act from what and who we actually are. Anyone who becomes aware that they are dreaming when awake or when asleep has a feel for both the dance of awareness and the dance of dreaming. Through dreams when we are sleeping, as we experience through meditation, we become much more responsive, fluid, and adaptable. We learn to not hold our experience with rigidity but with inquiry and exploration.

In sleeping dreams, our consciousness tells us, *Perhaps it is possible to be in two places at once. Perhaps it is possible to fly. Let's experiment and see.* It is this attitude of radical possibility that we can bring into daily life through conscious relationship with our dreams and imagination.

When I was a young person seeking alternatives to the greed and over-consumption I witnessed in our world, my capacity to dream bigger was deeply inspired by both the natural world and the indigenous peoples for whom I advocated in my nonprofit work at the time. For instance, the Ladakhi peoples, a Buddhist society in Northern India, did not have a poorhouse in their entire village until the introduction of industrialization in the 1970s. Nor did they have a word for rape because rape was not part of their collective dream. They existed in a strikingly harmonious paradigm and way of life, prioritizing kindness and partnership with nature in the stories they passed down through the generations, until the forces of global capitalism began to influence and disrupt their way of life.[11]

*   *   *

MINDFUL INQUIRY

How have nocturnal dreams offered significant guidance, support, direction, and healing in your life? In what ways do you bring consciousness to your nocturnal dreamworld? How might it support you to bring greater consciousness to your nocturnal dreamworld?

What is an experience that stands out to you, where the illusory nature of "ordinary reality" became especially clear? Perhaps you had a meditative experience where you became aware of your spiritual body extending far beyond your physical body. Or perhaps you had an experience of palpable communication with a form of life you had not communicated with before. How have you integrated the teaching of this experience into your everyday life?

* * *

EXPERIENTIAL PRACTICE: ACTIVE USE OF THE IMAGINATION

This is a partner practice. The person who is speaking first will begin by closing their eyes and thinking of a meaningful life memory, one that evokes joy. The speaker will allow all their senses to engage while sharing, out loud with eyes closed, the vivid sensory details of this experience. This can include the exact temperature, colors, sounds, tastes, and especially how it felt in their body-mind-heart. The listener will do nothing but listen. Then the pair will pause and switch roles.

After both people have shared, engage in a second round. This time, the practice will focus on a "future memory" or imagined future that evokes joy. This is an opportunity to literally dream out loud, in detail, while noticing how it feels to do so. Consider how it feels to be witnessed as you use your imagination? How does it feel to witness another as they dream out loud?

You can also engage in this practice with the following powerful prompt: Think of and actively imagine a future reality in which humans are living in a paradigm of kindness, sustainability, equity, and regeneration. How would it look and feel to live in this future reality?

* * *

EXPERIENTIAL PRACTICE: REMEMBERING DARKNESS
IN THE LIGHT OF DAY

The intention of this walking meditation practice is to consciously bring the darkness into our daytime awareness. This can help us to integrate our dreaming and waking life as a unified field. If you are a wheelchair user, you can let go of the walking aspect of this practice and engage from a seated position.

Begin by feeling your feet making contact with the ground beneath you. Take three slow mindful steps. Pause and close your eyes. Imagine that you are completely surrounded by darkness—in front of you, behind you, above you, below you, and on both sides. The place where you are was completely dark just hours ago, as it will be again when the night comes. Notice how it feels to give your eyes a rest from the visual field and allow your other senses to open. Let the darkness remind you of the spaciousness that is the backdrop of every moment. Let the darkness remind you of all that is unformed and invisible. Let the darkness remind you to honor your dreaming body and subconscious alongside your daytime existence. Let the darkness remind you that the relative world is never set in stone and that there is choice/possibility for you in every moment. Notice how it feels to remember this.

Then gently open your eyes, and with eyes open, allow yourself to sense the still-remaining presence of darkness surrounding you. Take three more mindful steps, and once again, pause and close your eyes.

What do you notice? Consider whether you can pause more often in your everyday life to allow the conscious mind and dreamer to integrate. Can you let your orientation soften to include even more wonder, receptivity, and curiosity about what you perceive as reality?

10

Cultivating Courage on Behalf of Life

Releasing Fear and Embracing Emergence

We need to move: from a spirituality of alienation from the natural
world to a spirituality of intimacy with the natural world.

THOMAS BERRY[1]

IN CHAPTER 1, I INVITED you to approach endarkenment through the
metaphor of walking off-trail through a dense forest—anchored in your
body, not knowing, listening deeply, and attuning within and out. As there
is no existing human-made trail for understanding darkness, heart-based
inquiry and receptivity are our most vital guides. Recognizing that no
brightly lit path with signs can direct us through spiritual evolution or
global uncertainty, I believe endarkenment can help to refine our inner
and collective compass. These teachings can help us to see more clearly—
from our hearts—in the dark. Please reflect on the ways you have given

yourself to befriending the dark. Or perhaps, through the chapters of this book, you have fallen in love with the dark, as I have in my life.

Humans have forever purposefully and intentionally walked through the darkness. We have traversed down into prehistoric caves and grottoes in the spirit of discovery and communion. We have rested in expanded awareness under the rejuvenating night sky. Darkness has invited us into the deeper recesses of dreaming and journeying beyond our daytime senses. Darkness has continually beckoned us to find out who we are on the other side of the threshold of fear.

Beyond choosing to commune with darkness, we have also always had experiences where the light went out suddenly—and we were left to face vulnerability and impermanence. In the final phase of writing this book, as I was working diligently to meet my deadline (a conventional phrase that I have always found humorous), my community was hit by a hurricane. In the four years my husband and I had lived in this area, we had never witnessed such torrential and electric rains. The power went out for an extended period. The creek shapeshifted into a rushing river. A large lake formed in our yard. Trees fell. Somewhat protected by the mountains, our home did not flood, nor did we have to evacuate, but major flooding occurred in our town, and neighbors evacuated.

The night of the storm, my husband and I sat in the dark with a couple of lit candles and listened to the rain pounding on the roof. Safe in our home, captivated by the thunder and lightning, we experienced both thrill and fear in the magnitude of the deluge.

Our feelings were already raw and tender. We felt helpless about a sangha member in the hospital ICU with COVID-19, unable to breathe. We felt absolute shock and heartbreak about the plight of the Afghan people, as the Taliban took over their country so quickly once the United States pulled out. It had already been a summer of onslaught from fires, floods, and the pandemic wreaking havoc globally. We were heartbroken by the reports from Haiti, so drastically devastated by earthquakes, flooding, and social upheaval.

The next morning the storm had passed, and the sun quickly rose high. With the power and internet still out, and without phone connection, we stepped outside and took a walk through the storm-strewn hills of the area where we live. Years ago, we had witnessed the entire refuge of Matilija Canyon in Ojai, California, dramatically reshaped and formed by fire, flood, and mudslides. The ancient rock formations, trees, and earth itself had gone through an almost complete metamorphosis. This storm had been less dramatic but still carried a sense of shock and sacred renewal at the same time. It was one of those experiences, for me, of being reminded so palpably about what matters and what does not. Book deadlines and email communications did not seem to matter.

Unable to go about our usual business, we slowly wandered the landscape, moving fallen branches, connecting with neighbors to support one another with kindness and share news. We gave ourselves to bringing care to our land, our garden, and our home after the storm. We were reminded that we had absolutely no control over external circumstances but absolute choice about the degree of love, presence, and sensitivity we brought forth. This felt significant, as we are all navigating a traumatized world. We were reminded that the recognition of impermanence continually feeds our commitment to embodying joy.

I believe that all of us are feeling raw and tender about the acceleration of climate change that has begun to take physical form. All of us are saddened, I believe, by the tear in the fabric of human relationship we have witnessed in recent years. I know the epidemic of divisiveness is beyond anything that has been experienced in my lifetime. The presence of fear in the collective psyche and the lack of psychological-emotional support for addressing such major global challenges have begun, I believe, to show up in collective psychic tension and further polarization.

As we navigate change, there is immeasurable value to spending time in darkened stillness. We need to slow down enough to feel and metabolize our anger, despair, and grief about what is already lost and can't be retrieved. We must find ways to see one another more clearly and to work together across borders, boundaries, and belief systems to help heal the only earth we have.

Inch-Wide Mile-Deep Movements

I love the idea of shifting from "mile-wide inch-deep" movements to "inch-wide mile-deep" movements that schism the existing paradigm.

ADRIENNE MAREE BROWN[2]

Years ago, I had the unique experience of living and farming at Arcosanti, the visionary urban ecovillage created in Arizona by architect Paolo Soleri. Both futuristic and antediluvian at the same time, Arcosanti exists in a dry and rocky desert, under the endless southwestern sky. To operate an organic farm in this desert landscape, we practiced creative and intelligent ways to collaborate with and use the resources we had. Many of the techniques we practiced came from traditional ways of farming.

A farmer from a nearby Hopi community shared their traditional way to plant corn seed. Rather than using the usual two-inch depth I was trained in to grow corn, the Hopi planted corn seed twelve inches deep to ensure solid protection in the dark topsoil from the seemingly endless sun. When the monsoons arrived in dramatic torrential downpours of rain, the seeds received the deep watering needed to finally sprout and grow deep roots in the soil. The Hopi traditionally sang to their seeds and seedlings joyfully and sweetly throughout the entire growing season. The vibrant colors and unique tastes of Hopi corn seemed to reflect, to me, the love and celebration that went into their unique process of cultivation.

The experience of organic farming itself built into my life purpose a focus on *process* rather than *product*. In the same way, *meditation practice* taught me to devote myself to *process* over *product*, to be present for the ever-emerging unfolding moment-by-moment process of being alive. Practice teaches us to orient through our direct experience of what is happening *now* rather than dilute our attention and energy with stories of the future and past. In the present we access a community of relationships that includes but is not limited to our human family.

Conventional farming has wreaked havoc on the earth, depleting and degrading topsoil, wasting and poisoning water sources, and contributing to global greenhouse gas emissions through a focus on product and speed—among many other forms of harm. Organic farming focuses on growing not the most produce the fastest but growing healthy regenerative soil. This is the black humus from which all substantial things grow. This soil is in itself a healthy community and ecosystem of myriad forms of life cooperating to sustain and regenerate life over time.

Practice is a metaphorical and metaphysical journey of cultivating healthy soil and sowing seeds of change. Awakening is not about the end goal, though the degree of freedom, compassion, vibrant aliveness, shared power, relational intelligence, and multinatural awareness that one reclaims as a result of practice is a treasure of immeasurable dimensions. Similar to the organic farmer, practice teaches us to devote ourselves to cultivating healthy regenerative soil in our lives. All of the nutrients provided within the human experience, the light and dark, joy and grief, ecstasy and decay, and ease and frustration are metabolized, composted, and integrated to nourish this soil. This soil generates continually more clarity, depth, and the distillation of love that is our birthright.

While the conventional farmer, in the spirit of marketplace mentality, focuses on horizontal growth, or "mile-wide" growth, the organic farmer/ spiritual practitioner is seeking depth, integrity, and quality of life experience for all. There is a rhythmic feeling of well-being to the process of preparing a garden bed, planting seeds, and composting. There is a well of joy in the experience of harvesting seed, saving seed, and in giving nutrients back to the soil to replenish it. This is the joy in serving life and participating in the coemergent process of our universe.

In the context of climate change and global uncertainty, we have a choice in every moment to honor our place on Earth by celebrating *emergence*. Rather than asking ourselves what we can do and feeling overwhelmed by not knowing, we can each participate in inch-wide, mile-deep movements every day of our lives. We can nourish the web of sacred relationships by showing up present and willing to work with exactly the resources we already have. Endarkenment reminds us to give ourselves to the fierce compassion and relational intelligence that feed mile-deep, inch-wide movements.

Imagine one person going through the actions of seed planting with fear and distress as their companion. Frightened by the threat of starvation, anxious that the rain won't come, terrified of future loss, they push the seed into the soil so distracted by fear that they are not actually engaged in what they are doing. Projecting loss and expiration onto life, they are, in essence, killing themselves while living life. This is the impact of clinging to fear in the face of the unknown.

As an alternative, imagine the farmer who is present and relaxed in their body, feeling gratitude for the earth as they give the seed to the soil, singing lovingly to the seeds, reveling in the human experience of watering the earth, opening to the wonder innate in seed sowing. The farmer is engaged in the process of growing corn, not worrying in this moment whether or not the rains will come so the corn can grow. Hoping, perhaps, to use some of the corn for seed and some for baking bread, they are giving themselves wholeheartedly to growing life. They are living fully, pouring themselves into nourishing the web of interconnection.

This is a metaphor for my lived experience of practice. Being human is a difficult experience. These are arduous times beyond what any of us can fathom. To devote ourselves to clear seeing and nourishing wholeness *in every moment* is how we serve the living systems of our planet. We have what it takes to navigate and integrate change wisely.

My favorite quote by Suzuki Roshi speaks directly to this: "When you do something, you should do it with your whole body and mind; you should be concentrated on what you do. You should do it completely, like a good bonfire. You should not be a smoky fire. You should burn yourself completely. If you do not burn yourself completely, a trace of yourself will be left in what you do."[3]

Returning to the metaphor of planting corn, picture the rain falling equally on adjacent fields, both comprised of the same seed and soil. One field was cultivated with the mindset of fear and one with pleasure and gratitude. Is there human influence and outcome from paying attention, singing to the corn, and praising the sun? Which farmer made more centered choices that benefited the whole? We can each look to our own experience and know with absolute certainty which cornfield grows better.

Practice allows the awareness of impermanence and death to continually feed our willingness to live. To truly live. It is our recognition of Kali, the dark Hindu goddess of destruction, that feeds our vibrant aliveness. We can each take responsibility for the process we bring to this time and to the quality with which we respond to global change. To recognize the wholeness that exists right now, in each moment, even alongside tragedy, is a radical act and contribution.

Committing to joyful presence is not selfish. It is not a spiritual bypass. It is an expression of mile-deep, inch-wide transformation. Dharma teaches that we are creating the world we choose to live in moment by moment. We take responsibility for our impact and make our offering for and with all beings, for and with our ancestors, for and with all forms of life. *It is resting in the refuge of well-being and interdependence that we receive insight and guidance, directly from the dark, on how to be of service.* I believe that our movements toward systemic change need to be based in relational intelligence to be powerful.

Focus Not on What Has Been Lost but on Emergence

We cannot navigate what lies ahead of us through the internal imbalance of rationalization, reactivity, distraction, fear, or the sense that we are separate. Our relationships are our greatest strengths.

There can, however, be overemphasis in human consciousness about what has been lost. We hold tremendous grief, for instance, about what we know and imagine certain ancient and indigenous peoples understood that we can no longer access. Although our grieving hearts and feelings cannot—and should not—be bypassed, we can also remember and embrace emergence. Our focus must be not on what has been lost, but in who we are now.

The simple architecture of darkened stillness, the subtle body, and our connection with the earth is all we need to remember who we are beyond fear. All fear is fear of loss. And in every moment that we give our attention to fear, we experience direct loss.

An example of this truth is the imminent and current threat of climate change. Our changing climate is a direct result of the use of fossil fuels due, in part, to the overlighting of our planet. Throughout the last few centuries and increasingly into this new century, the impacts of colonialism, capitalism supported by slavery, extraction of natural resources from indigenous lands, and the destruction of rainforests continue to detrimentally impact the survival of the human race, especially racial and ethnic minorities.

Although there have been studies and information about the threat and dangers of climate change for decades, there has been no significant change in how we live. The template we have for life does not include global warming. Not one of us evolved for this; so even wise beings who have a vision to end fossil fuels and reverse population growth have no clear strategy for implementation. Feeling so overwhelmed can make it easy to give in to terror, paralyzing despair, hopelessness, and finger-pointing outrage. It can be easy to bury our fear in a "business as usual" or "Pollyanna" avoidance approach. As an alternative, we can open our hearts to the complex and unfathomable dimensions of what is unfolding and commit to meeting it with love and awe.

Emergence Is the Organizing Principle of the Universe

Emergence as a phenomenon is the guiding story of Gaia. Over three million years ago, molecules of carbon and oxygen organized themselves into living cells, creating the first living entities or biological life. Through many mass extinctions and climate shifts over time, the slate has been wiped clean and most of what has been before has gone—and new patterns have emerged. Rather than focusing on what was lost from the Ice Age, what was lost when a giant meteor slammed into the Earth and created mass extinction, we can recognize that change is not the end of something. Through emergence, something new is always created. After the Ice Age, glaciers melted and there existed nothing but rock. From the air emerged spores of magical fungi. Algae and fungi made lichens and began to break down the rock. In the blink of the biological eye, there were plants forming and growing.

Emergence places us in the present moment. Today, we are not just experiencing the potential annihilation of our species—and the loss of what makes human life worth living, like forests and rivers—but we are also experiencing emergence. Emergence is current and can free us from our paralyzing grief and attachment to the past and future. Emergence is happening now and is the understanding that is most helpful as we navigate global climate change. *The projection into future and past keeps us locked in fear and unconsciousness.*

By recognizing that we are part of the emergence that is happening now, through inner and outer awareness, we can ask the following:

- What is emerging in our world in this moment? What is emergent in my consciousness when I listen deeply within and remain present to life's process? What is awakening within me?
- What qualities of wonder and respect for the mystery reawaken in my heart when I recognize emergence, alongside my grief for what is changing?
- How is there room for both greater acceptance and greater commitment to being of service/taking action when I remember emergence? Where is my care and support needed? How can I contribute, for instance, to slowing down the effects of climate

change and to supporting those populations who are being impacted most directly and immediately by climate change?

- What gets inspired in me when I recognize my role as a contributor to emergence? Might I realize that my love for our world and contribution to the morphic field today matter?

Consciousness by means we cannot begin to fathom has an organizing principle. *Emergence is the natural state of life.*

Beyond Anthropocentricity Is Engaged Hope

The focus of contemporary spirituality must move beyond anthropocentricity to remembering ourselves as collaborators with life. We can hold with reverence the unformed future—the network and nexus forming itself. We can learn to live not for the story humans have created but to be a vessel for emergent vision. We can also, through our meditation practice, commit to being a voice for the earth consciousness that exists in our bodies beyond concept.

My life's path and work with thousands of people over the years has given me certainty that our hope lies in reconnecting with the half of our consciousness that we have rejected—darkness itself. Humans today are seeking a choice beyond the brightly illuminated world of passive consumerism, compartmentalization, and rationalization. There is a yearning for restoration and wholeness beyond the busyness, division, distraction, and polarization we have invested in.

As our world changes physically and sociopolitically, as more and more people are displaced or feel uprooted by the omnipresent insecurity of global uncertainty, we crave *home.* Home is not a physical place. Home is wholeness, the field that unifies. We crave the dark wilderness to which we all belong.

We long for greater depth and for knowing ourselves as part of the interdependent web of nature's intelligence. We long for an alternative to the hyperactive, hyperurban, and suburban consumer lifestyle. We long for balance and belonging. We long for the quality of presence that proves nothing is separate, that all is connected.

The overlighting of human consciousness has nearly worn us out and has almost decimated our planet. But the night remains the night. The receptivity and sensitivity of our bodies are intact. The mystery from which we all came and to which we will all return has not dissolved. Bringing greater reverence to the mystery has the power to dismantle our limited egoic structures and habits.

Neuroscience has proven that neuroplasticity is the nature of the human brain, and human consciousness is equally malleable and ever changing. Each of us impacts the morphic field through every action and thought. We do not know if we will be able to slow down climate change. We do not know how long it will take human consciousness to nurture the seeds being planted today to end systemic racism for our children and grandchildren. *We do know that we have a choice now and in every moment.* Awakening is not a path of progression. The Buddha taught that we must each take responsibility for our own liberation now.

History demonstrates that there were times of surprising, unexpected shifts in the morphic field of human consciousness. If we remember that we do not wake up in isolation, as the solo spiritual warrior, but together, we can commit to inspiring one another, holding each other accountable, and dreaming together. Our every action, choice, and thought impact the morphic field.

There were also times when shifts were occurring that we violently resisted emergence. During the Copernican Revolution, for instance, many people were killed for claiming that the Earth revolved around the sun rather than being the center of the universe. Giordano Bruno was burned at the stake because his suggestion that the sun was actually another star threatened the then-limited view of the universe. Bruno's statement at the time was, "I await your sentence with less fear than you pass it. . . . The time will come when all will see what I see. Maybe you who condemn me are in greater fear than I who am condemned."[4]

But Isn't Knowledge Power?

In *Braiding Sweetgrass*, Robin Wall Kimmerer writes, "Science lets us see the dance of the chromosomes, the leaves of moss, and the farthest galaxy. But is it the sacred lens of the Popol Vuh? Does science allow us to perceive the sacred in the world, or does it bend light in such a way as to obscure it? A lens that brings the material world into focus but blurs the spiritual is a lens of the people of wood. It is not more data that we need for our transformation to people of corn but more wisdom."[5]

It has taken contemporary science a long time to question the dualist Cartesian paradigm which has, for the past few centuries, viewed humans as innately separate from nature. We are just beginning to wake up to the realization that it is not just human life that is conscious, but that every form of life is animate. The animal, fungal, mineral, and vegetal worlds are intelligently responding to their surroundings at all times. As many of you have experienced, these forms of life are ready to operate in partnership with humanity in the name of healing, the moment we open the door. Restoring our kinship with the web of life is what we need to evolve in partnership with nature.

In the words of the author Richard Powers, "It could be the eternal project of humankind, to learn what forests have figured out."[6]

Humanity is fatally shortsighted. When humans separated from nature and began to label, own, and apply hierarchical frameworks to the world around them, systems were established that evolved into governance and exploitation of the many by the few. The impact over centuries has been the careless destruction of ecosystems, global systemic racism, religious persecution, and grave disconnect within the fabric of human relationships.

Throughout human history, knowledge has been portrayed as light, and ignorance has been portrayed as darkness. We think of someone blindly stumbling around in the darkness of ignorance. We have abandoned our bodies to climb a mental ladder in search of illumination. We might have a mental/conceptual fixation with our bodies and physique, but that has nothing to do with embodiment. It is as if we think that by labeling and categorizing the entire world around us, we might gain a better understanding of life. But what does this knowledge actually serve? Has it not become an encyclopedia stored in a hidden chamber we use to subjugate and control? Has it not been used to support the myth that we are separate from life?

Our heart's desire is not to understand life but to know ourselves as nonseparate awareness itself. This remembrance of love includes the hundreds of thousands of species of love. This is our true nature.

Like any addictive activity, we distract and fill ourselves with information. Knowledge never fully satiates us. Knowledge is not the mighty lamp that gives us power. Presence restores the shared power by waking us up to nonseparation.

The Overlighting of Consciousness and the Brightly Lit Screen

We know well the impact of the physical overlighting of our planet. We know, for instance, that constant illumination harms the migration of nocturnal birds that are dying at an alarming rate. To move civilization forward, we must consider the harm caused by the overlighting of human consciousness. Instead of gathering around a sacred fire in community each night, many of us stare at a flickering screen without realizing that we can make other choices. Many people get so distracted by their emails and text communications that they are much less available for face-to-face and heart-to-heart conversations.

To enter into a conversation about the internet and computers, we need to evoke a shared understanding that from the perspective of dharma practice, attention is our greatest currency as human beings. Meditation practice is a training in using the currency of our attention wisely. When we give our attention to the mind of separation, we forget who we actually are.

The screen is certainly interesting and entertaining. We can honor and enjoy the source of entertainment and information that it is. We can acknowledge with boundless gratitude the ways it can support connection and interpersonal engagement—coming together for dharma practice online, for instance. We can appreciate the ways it supports those who are homebound, the disabled, and those who are otherwise isolated and alone. It allows more people than ever to work from home. It certainly helped many of us to survive through the pandemic. The benefits also depend, however, on how we spend our time on the screen.

Upon investigation, we might notice the many ways the screen seduces our attention. The backlit rectangle can touch every button of desire in our psyche, but can it really feed the embodied feeling of intrinsic wellness? The internet is sometimes the mental equivalent of junk food. It does not actually nourish our vitality, but it can occupy our attention for very long periods of time.

It is through embodied awareness that we stay connected to ourselves and each other. Fear marinates in the corners of our psyches dedicated to past and future, while presence positions us for emergent collaboration with life. If we were to be mindful of our quality of attention, then perhaps we would choose to enjoy the screen with greater moderation. Perhaps we would commit to practicing subtle body awareness while engaging with the screen. Perhaps we would support our youth to learn to have a mindful relationship with the screen. Like consuming a dessert, such as cheesecake, we may still choose to enjoy it—but not every day. We might acknowledge, through listening to our bodies, that it is not a wise choice to eat rich sugary foods every day.

The internet also conditions us to accept external authority—often supplanting our own internal authority. In a masterful stroke of subterfuge, by grabbing our attention and keeping us attentive to the screen, our personal interests are reflected back to us constantly. In addition, every action and choice we make is packaged and sold as data, which is a humiliating assault on the human spirit.

The morphic field holds a great deal of the dense and sticky conscious-ness of the victim and the passive consumer. Humankind misunderstands itself, believing in victimhood as a solid condition and believing in pas-sivity and consumption as a purpose. Humans also experience and allow ourselves to be producers. But producers of what? Increasingly, it seems to me that we have become producers of monetized increments of data. Even if we are not all consciously aware of this, this collective movement cannot be satisfying to the soul.

Over the past decade, the overlighting of human consciousness has hit a peculiar and unprecedented momentum. While we think that our rela-tionship with screens, data, and the internet has revolutionized our lives, the opposite may be true. *Data* translates to "facts and statistics collected together for reference or analysis." *Data* means "things known or assumed as facts, making the basis of reasoning or calculation."

What is the impact, psychospiritually, of perceiving our value based on the data that we produce for whatever purpose the forces who harvest that data choose? Are we not designing our world globally to serve the para-digm of logic and marketplace mentality? Is this the paradigm we want to evoke for our children? Are we not allowing ourselves to be harvested and mined the way pristine forests and deposits of minerals are mined? In other words, the data that each of us generates is used to feed global corporate capitalism.

While this might sound dramatic to some, I propose that this is akin to each person agreeing that "I am a hen in a factory egg farm. I produce what someone else profits from. That is my purpose in life." Of course, human beings can only be used for data in this way if we agree to be *pro-ducers* of data.

Some are starting to see the shadow side of the factory farming of human consciousness. In service to a marketplace mentality, human con-sciousness is being turned into a commodity the same way modern agri-culture turned plants into a commodity.

From Shortsightedness to Clear Seeing

We might sometimes reflect and recall that the purpose of all our
science, technology, industry, manufacturing, commerce, and finance is
celebration, planetary celebration. This is what moves the stars through
the heavens and the earth through its seasons. The final norm of judgment
concerning the success or failure of our technologies is the extent to
which they enable us to participate more fully in this grand festival.

THOMAS BERRY[7]

Humanity lacks long-term vision. When we began building large dams
across the planet, we could not have known that the weight of the dams
could cause a wobble in the Earth's axis. We could not have known that
our desire to tame rivers and harness their force for power would impact
the geophysical field of our planet. When we launched the Green Revolution, offering hybrids seeds and fertilizers to developing nations, we did
not envision the long-term repercussions, as traditional farming cultures
and livelihoods were destroyed. Rather than solve global famine and over-
population, the Green Revolution resulted in global soil degradation, a
damaged water table, a pesticide crisis, and massive social upheaval. Ironically, the Green Revolution caused the world's population to skyrocket
and world hunger to remain entrenched. When we first began using fossil
fuels for energy, we did not understand that this might lead to global climate change. We considered fossil fuels to be the modern technology that
would promote greater progress.

The healing of our world calls for emergent vision rather than short-
sightedness. This means that each one of us must look deeper. We are
invited to face our discomfort with stepping beyond conditioning. We
are invited to engage together in honest and healing conversations, even
if they feel difficult, to nourish understanding and collaboration. We are
required to open to guidance from beyond our limited minds. We are each

asked to put the manual aside, along with the whole library of manuals, expectations, and demands that keep humankind from clear seeing. Original consciousness and innate wisdom exist within each and every one of us and as a collective.

When I was a college student studying climate change in 1990, I felt devastated to the core by the socioenvironmental crises we faced even then. There was no support for my heartbreak over what I was learning about— and I felt fear, grief, despair, and outrage. Through meditation practice, the wisdom of my body, and my continual communion with the natural world, I began, step-by-step, to walk a regenerative journey of endarkenment.

Over the years, I have given myself to a path of communing with the divine darkness—through formal and informal practice—and this will continue throughout my life. Sometimes this has meant gently dipping my toes into the midnight sea of groundlessness, following a tiny tendril of courage even in the presence of fear. By doing so, I've learned continually that it is by *turning toward* rather than away from what I've labeled "dark," that my inner light is strengthened. To *turn toward* strengthens my discomfort resiliency and reawakens my courage.

Sometimes communing with the divine darkness has meant being willing to be more generous with myself than I have ever been before—setting aside the busying domain of daylight for deep immersions in the incubation, serenity, and regeneration my heart longed for. This has included meditation and shamanic practice, dreamwork, radical unapologetic rest, and darkness retreats.

Other times, communing with the divine darkness has meant calling upon the courage of every cell in my body and every ally I have—in the visible and invisible realms—to access a degree of shared power that terrified the small self. To navigate and heal that which completely overwhelmed me, there were times when fierce compassion required everything I had. It required me to call upon the tenacity of the tantric goddesses Kali, Black Tara, and Ekajati. It required me to call upon nature's might, letting Gaia's fierce, volcanic, earth-shaking energy move through me to shape me into a larger expression of love, vitality, and truth. It meant surrendering myself completely to the ecstasy and rapture that celebrates the potential of embodiment.

Endarkenment is a path of joy—the joy of knowing our shared power through the full spectrum of light and dark. Giving my life to practice has meant wholeheartedly pouring myself into what I love, completely, and letting it nourish the world in which I live. We can learn to trust that love is enough. We can learn not to hold back or limit the forms love can take. And we can receive the nourishment of our love in return.

I have learned that even in the face of fear, there can exist a tiny tendril of courage in our hearts. Without knowing exactly where we are headed, in each moment that we are willing to redirect our attention to this tendril and follow it, we are free. We are able to take the next step forward in service to life.

Our human existence is the full spectrum of light and dark, and we have what it takes to meet all of it with love. Because love is who we are.

If we are willing to take refuge in darkness more often, we can slow down our light speed to engage more wisely. Remembering that our heartbreak and love are two sides of the same coin, we can bring joy and celebration to our response to the world. We can listen to our feelings together rather than fight over our opinions. And we can remember the balance that is needed nourishment for each one of us, between dark and light, yin and yang, receptivity and expressiveness, attunement and productivity—the integration of our body-heart-mind.

Darkness is the threshold to every emergent moment. I find great inspiration through recognizing our role as conscious participants in emergence.

The inquiry that can support us as we navigate collective change is as follows:

How can we allow our love for our world and for each other to guide us more deeply in this moment?

How can we communicate with our own hearts with greater devotion?
And with one another with more care? Are we willing to take respon-
sibility for our own biases and energetic impact on the whole?

Can we learn to stay anchored in our soft, compassionate, forgiving bod-
ies in order to affirm the unity that is more real than separation and
battle? Can we stabilize our recognition that who we are is awareness
itself?

And can we commit to practices that restore us all, so that we are posi-
tioned to love well and to create a more regenerative world?

Beyond the repetitive action of talking and thinking and talking and
thinking about climate change and what humans should do, can we
take our inquiry more deeply into our hearts and into the process we
bring to life? Action is not the only medicine needed here, as it is only
useful in balance with receptivity.

As expressed in the introduction, I acknowledge that the questions
I have asked us to explore in this book are questions that we can only
answer together. My hope is that this book has touched and inspired you
to *more clearly* recognize your own gifts and contribution to our collective
transformation in an age of global fragility.

*   *   *

MINDFUL INQUIRY

Reflect on a time when you have followed the tendril of courage in the presence
in fear. What supported you to choose courage in this situation? What did you
learn about yourself in this situation? Can you think of a current situation
that triggers fear and imagine yourself following the tendril of courage and
affirming, once again, who you really are?

What is emerging through you in this age of climate crisis? What feel-
ings and awarenesses are arising as you bear witness to climate change? What
insights and fresh directives are arising about the quality of presence you choose

to bring to life? How are you being called into conscious response—through internal shifts and ways of being? Through generous actions?

In what ways do you engage in "mile-deep inch-wide movements" in your day-to-day life? How is the quality of your presence, receptivity, and compassion part of your commitment to being a contribution to our world? How do you nurture healing or connection through the way you show up to your relationships and interactions?

*   *   *

EXPERIENTIAL PRACTICE: ALLOWING THE
DARK TO REVEAL OUR INNER LIGHT

This is a practice for witnessing/befriending our suffering without trying to solve or transcend it. Think of an area of suffering or struggle in your life. You might consider picking that unwanted thing that has been around for a long time— perhaps an emotional trigger that still arises despite years of practice. Pick something that you feel well-resourced enough to work with in this moment. Notice what arises in the realm of mind, body, and feelings as you consider: How much energy and life force has gone into trying to fix, improve, understand, or transcend this aspect of your life? How have you judged, attempted to solve, or even cut off this unwanted part of you? What do you believe it means about you that this aspect of suffering exists in your life?

Now allow yourself to consider letting go completely of trying to solve or fix this. Perhaps the thought of letting go brings relief. Or perhaps it stirs fear. Take in a deep breath and rest here, gently turning toward this suffering. This suffering is a part of you, but it is not the whole of you. What might shift for you when you accept the slow invisible process of spiritual growth this suffering has called forth? What if, every time this arises, you could remember to perceive this, too, as a teacher in the emergent process of love?

Now, prepare to close your eyes or put on a blindfold to rest in the dark for a few minutes. Visualize wrapping yourself in a soft warm comforting blanket of darkness. Imagine the exact feel and texture of this blanket. Allow the darkness to encircle you with kindness . . . reminding you how it feels to be held . . . reminding you of your place in the mystery.

Remember that you don't have to transcend this suffering. You don't have to understand it. This suffering is not proof that there is something wrong with you. Please rest in nonjudgmental witnessing. Perhaps you notice more spaciousness? Tenderness? Patience? Compassionate neutrality? How is your inner light revealed when you rest here and trust this as a teacher of love? How might you commit to meeting this part of you more fully in friendship?

Take all the time you need for this practice. It is, in fact, helpful to repeat many times. When you feel ready, open your eyes. Make any notes you would like to make.

NOTES

1. Redefining Darkness

1. Wendell Berry, "To Know the Dark," *New Collected Poems* (Berkeley: Counterpoint, 2012), 68.
2. *The Amazing World of Mycelium*, directed by Paul Stamets (SAND, 2018), www.youtube.com/watch?v=JpCERNXtvMA.
3. Eleanor Janega, "Dr. Eleanor Janega (Medieval Sexuality)," interview by Christopher Ryan, *Tangentially Speaking*, podcast audio, January 4, 2021, https://chrisryanphd.com/456-dr-eleanor-janega-medieval-sexuality/.
4. "Universe 101: Our Universe," National Aeronautics and Space Administration, accessed August 1, 2021, https://map.gsfc.nasa.gov/universe/uni_matter.html.
5. Sojun Ikkyu, *Wild Ways: Zen Poems of Ikkyū*, ed. John Stevens (Boston: Shambhala, 1995), 26.
6. Donna Read, director, *The Burning Times* (National Film Board of Canada, 1990).
7. Wikipedia, s.v. "Song of the Precious Mirror Samadhi," last modified December 27, 2019, https://en.wikipedia.org/wiki/Song_of_the_Precious_Mirror_Samadhi.

2. Befriending the Night

1. C.G. Jung, *The Red Book,* ed. Sonu Shamdasani, trans. Mark Kyburz, John Peck, and Sonu Shamdasani (W. W. Norton & Company, 2009), 270.
2. Rebecca Boyle, "Light Pollution Is Destroying the Environment—The Dark Side of Light," *The Atlantic*, September 24, 2019, www.theatlantic.com/science/archive/2019/09/light-pollution-destroying-environment/598561/.
3. The Free Dictionary Online, s.v. "darkness," accessed January 1, 2021, www.thefreedictionary.com/darkness.

4. Francesco Berna, Paul Goldberg, Liora Kolska Horwitz, James Brink, Sharon Holt, Marion Bamford, Michael Chazan, "Microstratigraphic evidence of in situ fire in the Acheulean strata of Wonderwerk Cave, Northern Cape province, South Africa," *Proceedings of the National Academy of Sciences*, 109 (20): E1215–20, May 15, 2012, www.ncbi.nlm.nih.gov/pmc/articles/PMC3356665/.

5. National Park Service: Thomas Edison National Historic Park, "The Electric Light System," February 26, 2015, www.nps.gov/edis/learn/kidsyouth/the-electric-light-system-phonograph-motion-pictures.htm.

6. Simon Buxton and Ross Heaven, *Darkness Visible: Awakening Light through Darkness* (Rochester, Vermont: Destiny Books, 2005), 21.

7. John Reynolds / Vajranatha, "Dark Retreat as Preparation for the Bardo of Dying," Dharma Wheel, August 1, 2010, www.dharmawheel.net/viewtopic.php?t=21625.

8. Buxton and Heaven, *Darkness Visible*.

9. Mantak Chia, "Darkness Retreat Article," March 20, 2002, www.mantakchia.com/darkness-retreat-article/.

10. Malidoma Patrice Some, *Of Water and the Spirit: Ritual, Magic, and Initiation in the Life of an African Shaman* (New York: Penguin Books, 1995), 175.

11. Buxton and Heaven, *Darkness Visible*.

12. Buxton and Heaven, *Darkness Visible*.

13. Takie Sugiyama Lebra, *The Japanese Self in Cultural Logic* (Honolulu: University of Hawai'i Press, 2004), 194.

14. The material presented here is largely inspired by and adapted from Buxton and Heaven, *Darkness Visible*.

15. Rainer Maria Rilke, "The Night." *Rilke's Book of Hours: Love Poems to God*, trans. Anita Barrows and Joanna Macy (New York: Riverhead Books, 1996), 57.

3. Fierce Compassion

1. Andrew Holecek, *Bardos in Everyday Life* (online course), https://academy.andrewholecek.com/p/the-bardos-in-everyday-life.

2. Carl Jung, *Alchemical Studies*, vol. 13 of the *Collected Works of C. G. Jung*, 2nd ed. (Princeton University Press, 1980), 347.

3. Lama Rod Owens, "Mourning Utopia: Letting Go of the Idealized Past and Leaning into the Truth of the Moment and Beyond," interview by

Deborah Eden Tull, *Mindfulness and Meditation Summit*, The Shift Network, May 19, 2020, video, https://youtu.be/JhiIw2j4_QQ.

4. Octavia E. Butler, *Parable of the Talents* (Seven Stories Press, 1998), 285.

5. Andrew Holecek, "What We Can Discover in the Dark Unknown," *Tricycle: The Buddhist Review*, June 28, 2019, https://tricycle.org/trikedaily/buddhist-death-practices/.

4. Entering the Twilight Temple

1. Debbie Ford, *The Dark Side of the Light Chasers: Reclaiming Your Power, Creativity, Brilliance, and Dreams* (New York: Riverhead Books, 1998), 21.

5. Seeing in the Dark

1. Barbara Taylor Brown, *Learning to Walk in the Dark* (New York: HarperOne, 2014), 16.

2. Eihei Dogen, *The Essential Dogen: Writings of the Great Zen Master*, ed. Kazuaki Tanahashi and Peter Levitt (Boulder, CO: Shambhala, 2013), xvii.

3. Thich Nhat Hanh, *Interbeing: Fourteen Guidelines for Engaged Buddhism* (Berkeley: Parallax Press, 1987).

4. This story has been passed down through oral tradition in Zen Buddhist circles.

5. "12 Profound Ken Wilber Quotes & Sayings," The Famous People, https://quotes.thefamouspeople.com/ken-wilber-4919.php.

6. Colleen Deatsman. *The Hollow Bone: A Field Guide to Shamanism*. Red Wheel Weiser, 2011.

7. Suzuki Roshi, *Zen Mind, Beginner's Mind: Informal Talks on Zen Meditation and Practice* (Boston: Shambhala, 2011), 21.

8. David R. Hawkins, *Power vs. Force* (Carlsbad, CA: Hay House Inc., 2014), 162.

9. Sheila Stubbs, *Birthing the Easy Way by Someone Who Learned the Hard Way*, 2nd ed. (Volumes Publishing, 2008), 16.

6. The Slow, Dark Processes

1. Gabrielle Roth, "The Spiritual Power of Dance," *The Huffington Post*, October 26, 2012, www.huffpost.com/entry/spirituality-dance_b_862226.

2. Donna Goddard, *The Love of Being Loving* (Bloomington, IN: Balboa Press, 2013), 67.

3. Joanna Macy, personal correspondence to author, August 24, 2021, referring to a similar part in her book *World as Lover, World as Self* (Berkeley: Parallax Press, 1991), 26.

4. Rob Stein, "The Human Microbiome: Guts and Glory—Finally, a Map of All the Microbes on Your Body," *All Things Considered*, podcast audio, June 13, 2012, www.npr.org/sections/health-shots/2012/06/13/154913334 /finally-a-map-of-all-the-microbes-on-your-body.

7. Embracing Change

1. Michel Feyoh, "57 Pema Chodron Quotes to Live a More Mindful Life," Happier Human, June 4, 2019, www.happierhuman.com/pema-chodron -quotes/.

2. "An Interview with Cynthia Occelli: Resurrecting Venus," *The Richard Brendan Show*, radio, 2013.

3. *Merriam-Webster Online*, s.v. "liminal," last updated August 15, 2021, www.merriam-webster.com/dictionary/liminal.

4. Thomas Moore, *Dark Nights of the Soul: A Guide to Finding Your Way Through Life's Ordeals* (New York: Avery, 2005), 13.

5. Janine M. Benyus, *Biomimicry: Innovation Inspired by Nature* (New York: Harper Perennial, 2002), 7.

6. Izumi Shikibu, *Women in Praise of the Sacred: 43 Centuries of Spiritual Poetry by Women,* trans. Jane Hirshfield (New York: Harper Perennial, 1995), 59.

7. Wikipedia, s.v. "Women in Buddhism," last modified August 21, 2021. https://en.wikipedia.org/wiki/Women_in_Buddhism.

8. bell hooks, *Understanding Patriarchy* (Washington Square Press, 2004).

8. Relational Intelligence

1. Sojun Ikkyu, *Crow with No Mouth: 15th Century Zen Master*, trans. Stephen Berg (Port Townsend, Washington: Copper Canyon Press, 1989), 49.

2. Moore, *Dark Nights of the Soul*, xvi.

3. Richard Paul Evans, *The Gift: A Novel* (New York: Simon & Schuster, 2007), 162.

4. Sojun Ikkyu, *Wild Ways: Zen Poems of Ikkyū*, 13.

5. Joanna Macy and Molly Young Brown, *Coming Back to Life: The Updated Guide to the Work That Reconnects* (New Society Publishers, 2014), 194–96.

6. Resmaa Menakem, *My Grandmother's Hands: Racialized Trauma and the Pathway to Mending Our Hearts and Bodies* (Las Vegas: Central Recovery Press, 2017), 120.

7. Ruth King, *Mindful of Race: Transforming Racism from the Inside Out* (Louisville, CO: Sounds True, 2018), 4.

8. *How We Get Along: The Diversity Study of England and Wales 2020* (Woolf Institute, 2020), www.woolf.cam.ac.uk/research/projects/diversity.

9. Octavia E. Butler, *Lilith's Brood: The Complete Xenogenesis Trilogy* (New York: Open Road Media, 2012), 23 of "Dawn."

10. *Merriam-Webster Online*, s.v. "facilitate," last updated August 24, 2021, www.merriam-webster.com/dictionary/.

9. Dreams, Possibility, and Moral Imagination

1. Margaret Abrams, "Toni Morrison Quotes: The Author's Most Inspiring Musings on Love, Power, and Freedom," *Evening Standard*, August 6, 2019, www.standard.co.uk/insider/celebrity/toni-morrison-quotes-the-author-s-most-inspiring-musings-on-love-power-and-freedom-a4206951.html.

2. Wikipedia, "Capitalist Realist," last modified April 1, 2022, https://en.wikipedia.org/wiki/Capitalist_Realism.

3. Thomas Berry, *The Great Work: Our Way into the Future* (New York: Crown, 2000), 170.

4. Christine J. Nicholls, "'Dreamtime' and 'The Dreaming': Who Dreamed Up These Terms?" *The Conversation*, January 28, 2014, https://theconversation.com/dreamtime-and-the-dreaming-who-dreamed-up-these-terms-20835.

5. Alessandro Casale, "Indigenous Dreams: Prophetic Nature, Spirituality, and Survivance," *Indigenous New Hampshire Collaborative Collective*, January 25, 2019, https://indigenousnh.com/2019/01/25/indigenous-dreams/.

6. Stephen Aizenstat, "Here's What These Ancient Cultures Believed about Dreams," *Dream Tending*, February 22, 2019, https://dreamtending.com/blog/what-do-dreams-mean-ancient-cultures/.

7. Andrew Holecek, "Nocturnal Meditations, Dream Yoga, and Sleep Yoga," interview by Deborah Eden Tull, *Mindfulness and Meditation Summit*, The Shift Network, May 26, 2020, video as also discussed in Holecek's book

Dream Yoga: Illuminating Your Life Through Lucid Dreaming and the Tibetan Yogas of Sleep.

8. Alan Richardson, "Darkness Visible: Race and Representation in Bristol Abolitionist Poetry, 1770–1810," *Romanticism and Colonialism: Writing and Empire, 1780–1830,* ed. Tim Fulford and Peter J. Kitson (Cambridge: Cambridge University Press, 1998).

9. Martin Buber, *Tales of the Hasidim* (New York: Schocken Books, 1991).

10. Thomas Berry, *The Great Work,* 175.

11. Conversation with Helena Norberg-Hodge, author of *Ancient Futures: Learning from Ladakh,* 1993.

10. Cultivating Courage on Behalf of Life

1. Thomas Berry, *The Sacred Universe: Earth, Spirituality, and Religion in the Twenty-First Century* (New York: Columbia University Press, 2009), 133.

2. adrienne maree brown, *Emergent Strategy: Shaping Change, Changing Worlds* (Chico, CA: AK Press, 2017), 25.

3. Sreechinth C, *Shunryu Suzuki's Words of Wisdom: Quotes of a Soto Zen Monk* (India: UB Tech, 2018), 24.

4. G. Aquilecchia, "Giordano Bruno," Encyclopedia Britannica, March 19, 2021, www.britannica.com/biography/Giordano-Bruno.

5. Robin Wall Kimmerer, *Braiding Sweetgrass: Indigenous Wisdom, Scientific Knowledge, and the Teachings of Plants* (Minneapolis: Milkweed Editions, 2015), 345.

6. Richard Powers, *The Overstory* (New York: W. W. Norton & Company, 2018), 285.

7. Thomas Berry, *The Dream of the Earth* (San Francisco: Sierra Club, 1988), 69.

BIBLIOGRAPHY

Abrams, Margaret. "Toni Morrison Quotes: The Author's Most Inspiring Musings on Love, Power, and Freedom." *Evening Standard*, August 6, 2019. www
.standard.co.uk/insider/celebrity/toni-morrison-quotes-the-author-s-most-inspiring-musings-on-love-power-and-freedom-a4206951.html.

Aizenstat, Stephen. "Here's What These Ancient Cultures Believed about Dreams." *Dream Tending* (blog), February 22, 2019. https://dreamtending
.com/blog/what-do-dreams-mean-ancient-cultures/.

Aquilecchia, G. "Giordano Bruno." Encyclopedia Britannica, March 19, 2021. www.britannica.com/biography/Giordano-Bruno.

Benyus, Janine M. *Biomimicry: Innovation Inspired by Nature*. New York: Harper Perennial, 2002.

Berna, Francesco; Goldberg, Paul; Horwitz, Liora Kolska; Brink, James; Holt, Sharon; Bamford, Marion; Chazan, Michael. "Microstratigraphic evidence of in situ fire in the Acheulean strata of Wonderwerk Cave, Northern Cape province, South Africa." *Proceedings of the National Academy of Sciences* 109 (20): E1215–20, May 15, 2012. www.ncbi.nlm.nih.gov/pmc/articles
/PMC3356665/.

Berry, Thomas. *The Dream of the Earth*. San Francisco: Sierra Club, 1988.

——. *The Great Work: Our Way into the Future*. New York: Crown, 2000.

——. *The Sacred Universe: Earth, Spirituality, and Religion in the Twenty-First Century*. New York: Columbia University Press, 2009.

——. *Thomas Berry: Selected Writings on the Earth Community*. Modern Spiritual Masters Series. Edited by Mary Evelyn Tucker and John Grim. Ossining, NY: Orbis Books, 2014.

Berry, Wendell. *The Selected Poems of Wendell Berry*. Berkeley, CA: Counterpoint, 1999.

Bogard, Paul. *The End of Night: Searching for Natural Darkness in an Age of Artificial Light*. Boston: Little, Brown and Company, 2013.

Boyle, Rebecca. "Light Pollution Is Destroying the Environment: The Dark Side of Light." *The Atlantic*, September 24, 2019. www.theatlantic.com/science /archive/2019/09/light-pollution-destroying-environment/598561/.

Brown, Adrienne Maree. *Emergent Strategy: Shaping Change, Changing Worlds.* Chico, CA: AK Press, 2017.

Brown, Barbara Taylor. *Learning to Walk in the Dark.* New York: HarperOne, 2014.

Buber, Martin. *Tales of the Hasidim.* New York: Schocken Books, 1991.

Butler, Octavia E. *Lilith's Brood: The Complete Xenogenesis Trilogy.* New York: Open Road Media, 2012.

———. *Parable of the Talents.* New York: Seven Stories Press, 1998.

Buxton, Simon and Ross Heaven. *Darkness Visible: Awakening Spiritual Light through Darkness.* Rochester, Vermont: Destiny Books, 2005.

C., Sreechinth. *Shunryu Suzuki's Words of Wisdom: Quotes of a Soto Zen Monk.* India: UB Tech, 2018.

Casale, Alessandro. *"Indigenous Dreams: Prophetic Nature, Spirituality, and Survivance." Indigenous New Hampshire Collaborative Collective*, January 25, 2019. https://indigenousnh.com/2019/01/25/indigenous-dreams/.

Deatsman, Colleen. *The Hollow Bone: A Field Guide to Shamanism.* San Francisco: Red Wheel Weiser, 2011.

Dogen, Eihei. *The Essential Dogen: Writings of the Great Zen Master.* Edited by Kazuaki Tanahashi and Peter Levitt. Boulder, CO: Shambhala, 2013.

Eliade, Mircea. *The Sacred and The Profane: The Nature of Religion.* Translated by Willard R. Trask. New York: Harcourt Brace & Co, 1963.

Ellison, Koshin Paley. *Wholehearted: Slow Down, Help Out, Wake Up.* Somerville, MA: Wisdom Publications, 2019.

Evans, Richard Paul. *The Gift: A Novel.* New York: Simon & Schuster, 2007.

Feyoh, Michel. "57 Pema Chodron Quotes to Live a More Mindful Life." Happier Human, June 4, 2019. www.happierhuman.com/pema-chodron-quotes/.

Ford, Debbie. *The Dark Side of the Light Chasers: Reclaiming Your Power, Creativity, Brilliance, and Dreams.* New York: Riverhead Books, 1998.

Goddard, Donna. *The Love of Being Loving.* Bloomington, Indiana: Balboa Press, 2013.

Hanh, Thich Nhat. *Interbeing: Fourteen Guidelines for Engaged Buddhism.* Berkeley: Parallax Press, 1987.

Hawkins, David R. *Power vs. Force.* Carlsbad, CA: Hay House Inc., 2014.

Holecek, Andrew. *Bardos in Everyday Life* (online course). https://academy
.andrewholecek.com/p/the-bardos-in-everyday-life.

———. *Dream Yoga: Illuminating Your Life Through Lucid Dreaming and the
Tibetan Yogas of Sleep.* Louisville, CO: Sounds True, 2016.

———. "Nocturnal Meditations, Dream Yoga, and Sleep Yoga." Interview by
Deborah Eden Tull. *Mindfulness and Meditation Summit.* The Shift Network,
May 26, 2020. Video.

———. "What We Can Discover in the Dark Unknown." *Tricycle: The Buddhist
Review,* June 28, 2019. https://tricycle.org/trikedaily/buddhist-death
-practices/.

hooks, bell. *Understanding Patriarchy.* New York: Washington Square Press,
2004.

"How We Get Along: The Diversity Study of England and Wales 2020." Woolf
Institute, 2020. www.woolf.cam.ac.uk/research/projects/diversity.

Janega, Eleanor. "Dr. Eleanor Janega (Medieval Sexuality)." Interview by Christopher Ryan. *Tangentially Speaking.* Podcast audio. January 4, 2021, https://
chrisryanphd.com/456-dr-eleanor-janega-medieval-sexuality/.

Jung, Carl. *Alchemical Studies.* Vol. 13 of *The Collected Works of C. G. Jung.* 2nd
ed. Princeton, NJ: Princeton University Press, 1980.

———. *The Red Book.* Edited by Sonu Shamdasani and translated by Mark
Kyburz, John Peck, and Sonu Shamdasani, 270. New York: W. W. Norton &
Company, 2009.

Kimmerer, Robin Wall. *Braiding Sweetgrass: Indigenous Wisdom, Scientific Knowledge, and the Teachings of Plants.* Minneapolis, MN: Milkweed Editions, 2015.

King, Ruth. *Mindful of Race: Transforming Racism from the Inside Out.* Louisville,
CO: Sounds True, 2018.

Lebra, Takie Sugiyama. *The Japanese Self in Cultural Logic.* Honolulu: University
of Hawai'i Press, 2004.

Lena, Lama. "Impermanence, Dharma, and Buddha Nature." Public talk. Rime
Centre, Kansas City, July 2017. Video. https://lamalenateachings.com
/impermanence-death-buddha-nature/

Lesser, Elizabeth. *Cassandra Speaks: When Women Are the Storytellers, the Human
Story Changes.* New York: Harper Wave, 2020.

"Light Pollution." International Dark-Sky Association. 2019. Accessed January
1, 2021. www.darksky.org/light-pollution/.

Luongo Cassidy, Cindy. "Life on Earth Depends on Natural Darkness." Public

talk. First United Methodist Church, Waxahachie, TX, June 2017. www
.inaturalist.org/posts/10473-life-on-earth-depends-on-natural-darkness.

Macy, Joanna. *World as Lover, World as Self*. Berkeley: Parallax Press, 1991.

Macy, Joanna and Molly Young Brown. *Coming Back to Life: The Updated Guide
to the Work That Reconnects*. Gabriola, BC, Canada: New Society Publishers,
2014.

Madrid, Aurelio. "Fundamental Darkness." *Luctor et emergo* (blog). May 27,
2009. https://aureliomadrid.wordpress.com/2009/05/27/fundamental
-darkness

Menakem, Resmaa. *My Grandmother's Hands: Racialized Trauma and the Pathway
to Mending Our Hearts and Bodies*. Las Vegas, NV: Central Recovery Press,
2017.

Moore, Thomas. *Dark Nights of the Soul: A Guide to Finding Your Way through
Life's Ordeals*. New York: Avery, 2005.

National Aeronautics and Space Administration. "Universe 101: Our Universe."
Accessed August 1, 2021. https://map.gsfc.nasa.gov/universe/uni_matter.html.

National Park Service: Thomas Edison National Historic Park. "The Electric
Light System," February 26, 2015. www.nps.gov/edis/learn/kidsyouth/the
-electric-light-system-phonograph-motion-pictures.htm.

Nicholls, Christine J. "'Dreamtime' and 'The Dreaming': Who Dreamed Up
These Terms?" The Conversation, January 28, 2014. https://theconversation
.com/dreamtime-and-the-dreaming-who-dreamed-up-these-terms-20835.

Nichtern, David. *Creativity, Spirituality, and Making a Buck*. Somerville, MA:
Wisdom Publications, 2019.

Owens, Lama Rod. "Mourning Utopia: Letting Go of the Idealized Past and
Leaning into the Truth of the Moment and Beyond." Interview by Deborah
Eden Tull. *Mindfulness and Meditation Summit*, The Shift Network, May 19,
2020. Video. https://youtu.be/JhiIw2j4_QQ.

"Patriarchy: A Primer for Men." The Nation. July 11, 2007. www.thenation.com
/article/archive/patriarchy-primer-men/.

Powers, Richard. *The Overstory*. New York: W. W. Norton & Company, 2018.

Read, Donna. Director. *The Burning Times*. National Film Board of Canada, 1990.

Richardson, Alan. "Darkness Visible: Race and Representation in Bristol Abolitionist Poetry, 1770– 810." *Romanticism and Colonialism: Writing and Empire,
1780–1830*. Edited by Tim Fulford and Peter J. Kitson. Cambridge: Cambridge University Press, 1998.

Rilke, Rainer Maria. "Let This Darkness Be a Bell Tower." *In Praise of Mortality: Selections from Rainer Maria Rilke's Duino Elegies and Sonnets to Orpheus.* Translated by Anita Burrows and Joanna Macy. Brattleboro, Vermont: Echo Point Books & Media.

———. "The Night." In *Rilke's Book of Hours: Love Poems to God.* Translated by Anita Barrows and Joanna Macy. New York: Riverhead Books, 1996.

Roth, Gabrielle. "The Spiritual Power of Dance." *The Huffington Post,* October 26, 2012. www.huffpost.com/entry/spirituality-dance_b_862226.

Safransky, Sy. *Sunbeams: A Book of Quotations.* Berkeley: North Atlantic Books, 1990.

Sheff, David. *All We Are Saying: The Last Major Interview with John Lennon and Yoko Ono.* New York: St. Martin's Griffin, 2000.

Shikibu, Izumi. *Women in Praise of the Sacred: 43 Centuries of Spiritual Poetry by Women.* Translated by Jane Hirshfield. New York: Harper Perennial, 1995.

Sojun, Ikkyu. *Crow with No Mouth: 15th Century Zen Master.* Translated by Stephen Berg. Port Townsend, Washington: Copper Canyon Press, 1989.

———. "Every day priests . . ." *Wild Ways: Zen Poems of Ikkyū.* Edited by John Stevens. Boston: Shambhala, 1995.

Some, Malidoma Patrice. *Of Water and the Spirit: Ritual, Magic, and Initiation in the Life of an African Shaman.* New York: Penguin Books, 1995.

Stamets, Paul. Director. *The Amazing World of Mycelium.* SAND, 2018. www.youtube.com/watch?v=JpCERNXtvMA.

Stein, Rob. "The Human Microbiome: Guts and Glory—Finally, a Map of All the Microbes on Your Body." *All Things Considered.* Podcast audio. June 13, 2012. www.npr.org/sections/health-shots/2012/06/13/154913334/finally-a-map-of-all-the-microbes-on-your-body.

Stubbs, Sheila. *Birthing the Easy Way by Someone Who Learned the Hard Way.* 2nd ed. Volumes Publishing: 2008.

Suzuki Roshi. *Zen Mind, Beginner's Mind: Informal Talks on Zen Meditation and Practice.* Boston: Shambhala, 2011.

Tudge, Colin. *The Secret Life of Trees.* New York: Penguin Press Science, 2006.

Tull, Deborah Eden. *Relational Mindfulness: A Handbook for Deepening Our Connections with Ourselves, Each Other, and the Planet.* Somerville, MA: Wisdom Publications, 2018.

Wohlleben, Peter. *The Hidden Life of Trees: What They Feel, How They Communicate—Discoveries from a Secret World.* Vancouver, Canada: Greystone Books, 2016.

ABOUT THE AUTHOR

Deborah Eden Tull, the founder of Mindful Living Revolution, is an engaged dharma teacher, public speaker, author, and activist. She spent seven years as a Buddhist monk at a silent Zen monastery and offers retreats, workshops, and consultations internationally. Eden teaches dharma intertwined with post-patriarchal thought and practices, resting upon a lived knowledge of our unity with the more than human world. Her books include *Relational Mindfulness: A Handbook for Deepening Our Connection with Ourselves, Each Other, and the Planet* (Wisdom 2018) and *The Natural Kitchen: Your Guide for the Sustainable Food Revolution* (Process Media 2011). Eden's teachings bridge the personal, interpersonal, transpersonal, ecological, cultural, global, and mystical impacts of awareness practice—drawing upon her embodiment of inquiry, deep ecology, relational intelligence, animism, and conscious movement/dance to help people release the myth of separation and reclaim the authority of the heart. She also teaches the Work That Reconnects, created by Buddhist scholar Joanna Macy for transforming our pain and love for our world into compassionate action. Eden lives with her husband in the mountains of Western North Carolina where she practices partnership with nature and Earth stewardship. Through her love of service, Eden feels a sincere commitment to you, the reader, and to all who wish to embody the teachings of *Luminous Darkness*. For more information, please visit deborahedentull.com.